The
Reference Shelf®

Food Insecurity & Hunger in the United States

The Reference Shelf
Volume 93 • Number 2
H.W. Wilson
A Division of EBSCO Information Services, Inc.

Published by
GREY HOUSE PUBLISHING
Amenia, New York
2021

The Reference Shelf

Photo courtesy of North East Community Center, Millerton, NY.

The books in this series contain reprints of articles, excerpts from books, addresses on current issues, and studies of social trends in the United States and other countries. There are six separately bound numbers in each volume, all of which are usually published in the same calendar year. Numbers one through five are each devoted to a single subject, providing background information and discussion from various points of view and concluding with an index and comprehensive bibliography that lists books, pamphlets, and articles on the subject. The final number of each volume is a collection of recent speeches. Books in the series may be purchased individually or on subscription.

Publisher's Cataloging-In-Publication Data
(Prepared by The Donohue Group, Inc.)

Names: Grey House Publishing, Inc., compiler.
Title: Food insecurity & hunger in the United States / [compiled by Grey House Publishing].
Other Titles: Reference shelf ; v. 93, no. 2.
Description: Amenia, New York : Grey House Publishing, 2021. | Includes bibliographical references and index.
Identifiers: ISBN 9781642657906 (v. 93, no. 2) | ISBN 9781642655995 (volume set)
Subjects: LCSH: Food security--United States--Sources. | Hunger--United States--Sources. | Food supply--United States--Sources. | LCGFT: Reference works.
Classification: LCC HD9005 .F66 2021 | DDC 363.80973--dc23

Printed in Canada

Contents

3

Finding Food

4

The World's Problem

5

Finding Solutions

Feeding the Masses

America's Food Crisis

America is not so much in the midst of a food crisis as in the midst of multiple food crises. Despite being the wealthiest nation in the world, millions of people in America struggle to get enough food or to afford high quality, nutritious food. Access to food and the quality of food available in various communities, cities, and towns is related to broader patterns of investment and infrastructure. It is largely a product of the corporatization of the American food industry. Coupled with wage stagnation and income inequality, the rising cost of food has meant that more Americans are unable to achieve a healthy diet. This leads to a variety of medical and mental health issues that place a further strain on individuals and families. On an even broader scale, climate change and global instability disrupts production, distribution, and cost and threatens to make access to food more problematic over the longer term.

A Core Dysfunction

In the Colonial era in America, nearly all the food that colonists ate was grown locally. From the Native Americans, the colonists learned to cultivate and to eat maize, sweet potato, tomatoes, pumpkins, squash, watermelons, beans, grapes, berries, pecans, peanuts, and many other foodstuffs still common across the Americas. However European agriculture was already a global endeavor. Common European crops like apples, peaches and grains like spelt and wheat were originally native to Asia before they were carried around the world to become key crops in Britain. Americans brought these same crops to the Americas, cultivating them alongside native crops. When it came to meat, the Americas provided a wealth of edible animals, from the thousands of species of fish in the seas, rivers, and lakes, to deer, buffalo, and hundreds of varieties of other wild game. The colonists also brought cattle, pigs, sheep, chickens, and goats to the new world and they cleared millions of acres of forests and prairies to establish grazing land.[1]

From the very beginning, food in America was not only used to sustain those who needed to eat but it also became the core of the new American economy. The trade in crops, flowers, and spices fueled the rise of empires and kingdoms, and the decision to establish the American colonies was part of the effort to marshal power in the global culinary trade. The nation's first successful colony in Jamestown, Virginia, was an economic endeavor, planned and executed by a corporation that wanted to profit. Exports of Native American crops like tobacco, potatoes, and corn fueled the rise of America's first wealthy elite class, while deepening the pockets of the British aristocracy as well. Men like Thomas Jefferson and George Washington became wealthy by utilizing slave labor to grow massive plantations that shipped crops like tobacco and hemp back to England as well as supplying the growing millions of colonial laborers.[2]

The corporate origins of American agriculture have dominated the nation's relationship to food ever since. In the colonies most food was grown locally. Without the ability to freeze and ship food over long distances, it was simply more practical to eat what was grown in one's immediate area. Many Americans lived as farmers and would eat what they were able to grow on their own farms, supplemented by food they purchased or traded at local and regional agricultural markets. While these early European Americans lacked culinary variety, their food was fresher and healthier than much of what Americans consume in the twenty-first century. Nevertheless, the distribution of food was anything but egalitarian.

While the Washingtons and Jeffersons of the New World were wealthy enough to eat the finest of what was available, many of those who arrived in the Americas left poverty in Europe to try their fortunes in the New World, or were forcibly transported as convict laborers or slaves. For individuals at the low end of the totem pole, affording food was tough. Cornmeal pudding, porridge, and potatoes made up the bulk of the diet for many in the working classes, who could not afford game or fresh vegetables. For those too poor to afford porridge, a watered-down version, known as "gruel," could be eaten to provide sustenance, but it had little nutritional value. Slaves were often fed gruel as well and forced to eat food of the same quality as that given to pigs and goats, left over agricultural products not suitable for sale.[3] The mortality rate among the poor, especially children, was high until recently in history. Fewer than half of American-born children survived to adulthood until well into the 1800s. Children, especially, suffered inordinately from poverty and famine in the early history of America.

The Industrial Revolution—which brought new advances in technologies related to food production, storage, and distribution—was the beginning of one of the most damaging inventions in the history of American life, processed foods.

As America became more complex and urbanized, many no longer had direct access to farms and markets where fresh products were sold. Obtaining food became more difficult and companies met this need with prepackaged foods. Meats, legumes, and vegetables were precooked, mixed with chemicals and "filler" ingredients, and then stored in cans. Cans could be stored for months, and the food only needed to be reheated rather than cooked. Convenience was the key goal for the early packaged food corporations, and they achieved this goal, but at the cost of quality and nutritional value. Precooked foods contain only a portion of the vitamins and minerals that would be found in fresh versions of those same foods. Companies increasingly began offering food items that were more "filler" than actual food. This enabled them to sell less product for higher cost, but this profit came at the expense of the health and welfare of the American people.[4]

Over time, companies learned that Americans respond more to flavor than to quality. By adding salt, sugar, and spices, companies marketed foods made from little more than agricultural waste. Packaged potato chips, grain cereals, and soft drinks require very little material to produce but remain popular because they carry strong flavors and textures. These foods can be extremely low in price. Those in the laboring class therefore increasingly depended on these low-quality foods. The success of low-quality packaged foods led to the growth of massive multi-state corporations, and these companies tended to put smaller markets, agricultural outlets, and independent grocers out of business.

While the processed food industry gradually replaced small-scale agriculture and food providers, Americans also imported more of their food products from overseas, as the cost of doing so was cheaper than the cost of producing foods locally. Mass agricultural programs in many countries increased the yield of crops by adding hormones and chemicals that increased growth rate but often had a deleterious impact on nutritional content as well. As these foods began to flood the American market, the quality of food declined across the entire spectrum so that even fresh vegetables purchased from a store might be laced with chemicals, insecticides, and hormones and might lack the nutritional value that the same basic food contained centuries earlier.[5]

Americans in the twenty-first century live in a food environment dominated by corporate profit and centered around the product of mass quantities of low-quality food products. This transformation has not gone unnoticed, and even in the early 1800s some Americans protested the food industry and campaigned to improve the quality of food. Ultimately, farmer's markets and health food stores emerged to counter the mass food market, and these outlets provided a way for Americans to still obtain high quality and fresh foods. However, as the cost of living increased and real wages stagnated, better quality foods became more difficult to afford and eventually became a niche market available primarily to the affluent. The drive for better and more "natural" foods ultimately led to the birth of corporations like Whole Foods and Wild Thyme, which marketed healthier, organic, and more nutritious options. While these chains began out of an earnest effort to counteract the declining quality of available mass-produced foods they became more corporate and succumbed too many of the same problems plaguing the mass grocery market as a whole.[6]

The Many Facets of a National Problem

America's food problem is ultimately part of a deeper problem, wage and income inequality. Between the ten 10 years since the Great Recession of 2008–09, proactive economic recovery policies enacted by the Obama administration helped to stem unemployment and led to an increase in absolute wages. But the gains that the economy made were not evenly shared. In 2020, the highest earning 20 percent of Americans made more than half of the nation's income combined. Over the past half century, this share of Americans, have increased their share of income dramatically. In 1968, for instance, the top 5 percent of wealthy Americans earned 16 percent of all income in the nation. By 2018, they earned nearly 23 percent. The gap in wealth between the rich and poor more than doubled over the years from 1990 to 2016 and middle- and working-class incomes have grown at an exceedingly slow rate. From 1970 to 2018, the median income for the middle class increased by 49 percent, while the income for the upper class increased by more than 64 percent.[7]

While absolute poverty has been falling, the number of Americans living in poverty continues to pose a major problem. In 2018, at least 38 million Americans lived in poverty, constituting nearly 12 percent of the American population. In the United States poverty is defined as having an income of around $26,000 or less for a family of four. Many of those living in poverty work more than one job but are unable to earn enough to pull themselves or their family out of destitution. Many are seniors on fixed incomes, individuals with medical issues that make it difficult to find gainful employment, or individuals who have been laid off from their jobs. Poverty affects more women than men and affects non-white individuals more than the white population. Native Americans, for instance, have a poverty rate of over 25 percent, while African Americans have a poverty rate of 20 percent, as compared to the 10 percent of white Americans who live in poverty.[8]

Beyond those classified as living in poverty, there are many whose incomes are just above the poverty line. The underemployed and even the average working-class family may struggle to afford even the most low-cost food available in their area; they typically cannot afford more nutritious or higher-quality foods. Millions live in what activists have termed "food insecurity," which means that while the individual or family might be able to afford food most of the time, doing so is a struggle, and they live in constant fear of being unable to afford the next meal.

There are state and federally subsidized programs that can help. Supplemental Nutrition Assistance Program (SNAP) benefits, otherwise known as "food stamps," are one of the most familiar of these programs, but there are a number of other regional and national programs. Parents in some municipalities can access programs that provide subsidized food for children, and many public-school systems have programs funded by government revenues that provide subsidized lunches for students. While such programs are well meaning, the level of nutrition provided is frequently inadequate, and programs in many states are insufficiently funded.[9] School lunch inequality not only deprives children of nutrition and continues a cycle of disadvantage, but it has become another factor influencing the social marginalization of students from lower-income families.

The phenomenon of the American "food desert," where residents of a certain area lack food options, is another of the major problems fueling hunger and food insecurity in America. Families and individuals who can only access or afford lower-quality foods suffer from higher rates of obesity, heart disease, and other disorders linked to malnutrition. Even when communities, developers, or activists manage to increase food options in certain areas, essentially eliminating the food desert problem, many families living in those areas often still lack the resources to afford better food options.[10]

A Broader Concern

Food inequality is not only a problem in America but in many nations around the world. In most cases, income inequality and wage stagnation are the chief underlying factors, but there are other contributing factors as well. Trade agreements and corporate supply chain decisions play a major role in determining what food is available in what areas. Corporations that supply much of America's food depend on exports and imports, and so global politics and economic shifts can impact America's food industry. Beyond this, as temperatures around the world have continued to rise, the climate has begun to experience frequent, violent changes. Tropical storms have become more common and more intense, while in other regions droughts and wild-fires have decimated communities and agricultural territories. Weather changes have led to insect and pest infestations, to poor crop yields, and to the collapse of whole farming regions. Because climate change is a global phenomenon, it impacts the entire global food industry. At the local and regional level, disturbances in agricultural production can lead to local famine, pushing already disadvantages families into destitution. Further, competition for dwindling supplies of water and food has the potential to instigate wars and social unrest. The ongoing war in the Sudan is, in part, motivated by a decade of drought, which has ignited tensions between groups struggling to obtain sufficient water and food to survive.

In 2019, the World Health Organization (WHO) estimated that there were more than 820 million around the world unable to obtain sufficient food for themselves or their families. This marked the third year in a row that food insecurity and hunger had increased, and WHO researchers noted also that climate change and related social/economic disturbances are not only increasing global hunger but accelerating the pace at which the marginalized fall into absolute poverty. As in America, rates of hunger and food insecurity are higher for women and children than for men, affecting the next generation and leading to a cycle of food insecurity and income inequality.[11]

Solutions and Resolutions

In the United States, specific legislative campaigns and community outreach programs aim to eliminate food deserts and to bring more nutritious food options to marginalized communities. There are campaigns for governmental reform focused on improving subsidies for struggling individuals, families, and school-aged children. There are citizen-led efforts to increase urban and local agriculture and to involve community residents in the process of creating and preparing their own food, and there are innovative new farming and food production techniques that might be used to defray some of the difficulties associated with mass agriculture.

America, like most nations, always faces serious problems, but the nation's greatest strength—the diversity and innovativeness of the American people—may well prove the key to handling the nation's hunger issues. For this to become a reality, however, Americans must prioritize these efforts and commit to breaking barriers that prevent citizens from thriving and creating a future of better food quality and access for all Americans.

Works Used

Davis, Joshua C. *From Head Shops to Whole Foods: The Rise and Fall of Activist Entrepreneurs*. New York: Columbia University Press, 2017.

Horn, James. *1619: Jamestown and the Forging of American Democracy*. New York: Basic Books, 2018.

McMillan, Tracie. *The American Way of Eating: Undercover at Walmart, Applebee's, Farm Fields and the Dinner Table*. New York: Scribner, 2012.

McWilliams, James E. *A Revolution in Eating: How the Quest for Food Shaped America*. New York: Columbia University Press, 2005.

Nunn, Nathan, and Nancy Qian. "The Columbian Exchange: A History of Disease, Food, and Ideas." *Journal of Economic Perspectives*, vol. 24, no. 2, 2010. https://scholar.harvard.edu/files/nunn/files/nunn_qian_jep_2010.pdf.

"The Population of Poverty USA." *Poverty USA*. 2020. https://www.povertyusa.org/facts.

The Public Health Effects of Food Deserts: Workshop Summary. National Research Council. Washington, DC: The National Academies Press, 2009.

Schaeffer, Katherine. "6 facts about Economic Inequality in the U.S." *Pew Research*. Feb 7, 2020. https://www.pewresearch.org/fact-tank/2020/02/07/6-facts-about-economic-inequality-in-the-u-s/.

Sweeney, Erica. "The Problem with School Lunch: How the Wealth Gap Is Shaming Students." *Huffpost*. Aug 20, 2018. https://www.huffpost.com/entry/school-lunches-wealth-gap_n_5b72ee42e4b0bdd0620d0b43.

Temple, Nicola. *Best Before: The Evolution and Future of Processed Food*. New York: Bloomsbury Publishing, 2018.

"World Hunger Is Still Not Going Down After Three Years and Obesity Is Still Growing—UN Report." *WHO*. https://www.who.int/news/item/15-07-2019-world-hunger-is-still-not-going-down-after-three-years-and-obesity-is-still-growing-un-report#:~:text=More%20than%20820%20million%20people%20are%20hungry%20globally&text=An%20estimated%20820%20million%20people,of%20increase%20in%20a%20row.

Notes

1. Nunn and Qian, "The Columbian Exchange: A History of Disease, Food, and Ideas."
2. Horn, *1619: Jamestown and the Forging of American Democracy*.
3. McWilliams, *A Revolution in Eating: How the Quest for Food Shaped America*.
4. Temple, *Best Before: The Evolution and Future of Processed Food*.
5. McMillan, *The American Way of Eating: Undercover at Walmart, Applebee's, Farms Fields and the Dinner Table*.
6. Davis, *From Head Shops to Whole Foods: The Rise and Fall of Activist Entrepreneurs*.
7. Schaeffer, "6 Facts about Economic Inequality in the U.S."
8. "The Population of Poverty USA," *Poverty USA*.

9. Sweeney, "The Problem with School Lunch: How the Wealth Gap Is Shaming Students."

10. *The Public Health Effects of Food Deserts: Workshop Summary,* National Research Council.

11. "World Hunger Is Still Not Going Down After Three Years and Obesity Is Still Growing—UN Report," *WHO.*

1

Poverty, Unemployment, and Underemployment

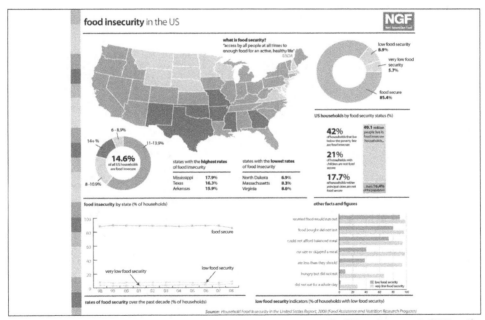

By Tiffany Farrant, via Wikimedia.

Food insecurity in the United States.

The Economic Dimension of America's Food Problems

One of the primary drivers of hunger and food insecurity is income. Individuals who live in poverty, those who live just above this level but are still underemployed, and even those who earn barely enough to cover their needs all face problems obtaining adequate food or, at least, adequate nutrition. Ultimately, food insecurity and hunger can be considered a dimension of the broader struggle with wealth.

The Income Inequality Problem

Despite being the wealthiest nation in the world, the United States also has the highest level of income inequality of the Group of Seven (G7) nations, an informally recognized group of trading partner countries that also includes France, Germany, Italy, Japan, the United Kingdom, and Canada.[1] The wealth of the United States and the nation's economic inequality are interrelated. America is wealthier than the other nations because it is a larger nation and rich in natural resources. If the United States was smaller, or if it had, like Canada, vast tracts of territory unsuitable for farming, the United States would not now be the wealthiest nation in the world.

The American people have also embraced a free market economic system that emphasizes personal wealth over public welfare. While free market capitalism is excellent for creating wealth, the degree to which capitalist systems benefit consumers depends largely on whether or not the members of that society can mitigate the impact of greed and can protect citizens trying to work their way through the system from those who have already amassed wealth and power.

Consider, for instance, the medical industry. American hospitals attract some of the finest medical students in the world because physicians can earn far more working in the United States than in many other countries and because the United States invests heavily in the medical industry. Although spending on medicine outpaces many other nations, the United States has some of the worst health outcomes in the Western world.[2] America's medical system works on a for-profit basis and so those without economic advantages receive lower quality medical care. Even individuals who are economically stable may be thrown into financial disarray by the high price of medical care if they encounter an unforeseen medical issue. By contrast, many other European nations have adopted socialized medical systems in which collective taxation pays for the nation's healthcare. The American system produces more top-tier physicians than medical systems in many allied Western nations but this high-quality healthcare is available disproportionately to the wealthy.[3]

For those who don't have access to inherited getting ahead in America can be very difficult. Since the 1970s, the wealthiest 20 percent of Americans have increased

3

their wealth nearly 60 percent, but income growth for the middle and lower classes has been stagnant. The wealth gap, which is the difference in compensation between the wealthiest and poorest families, has more than doubled since 1989. Studies have shown that the modest increases in income seen by those in the middle and working class have been insufficient to constitute real wage advancement. This means that purchasing power for the vast majority of Americans has either remained stagnant or has actually decreased since the middle of the twentieth century.[4]

Social scientists have completed many studies and economic analyses that suggest that the most significant issue affecting income mobility in the United States is unfair compensation. Corporate profits are primarily distributed to investors and upper management. Income rates at lower levels are frequently insufficient for an individual or family to accrue savings, invest in equity, or to engage in other measures that might ultimately allow them to advance within the income spectrum.

When it comes to combating hunger, wage stagnation is at the core of the issue. In twenty-first century America, affordable food tends to be processed and mass produced, and this kind of food also tends to lack nutritional value. As mass-produced food became the core of the American food market, nutritious and organic food options have increasingly become luxury goods. Because of wage stagnation, Americans in the working class have been priced out of access to quality food. Insufficient nutrition contributes to a wide variety of health and wellness issues, and this complicates the difficulties faced by those lacking resources in America. Hunger and the overall equity of the American economy are two sides of the same coin, and thus any effort to solve America's ongoing hunger problem is complicated by the overarching income inequality problem in the United States.

Underemployment

In America poverty is set at a level of $70 per day for a family of four. A family that earns $80 dollars a day may not be considered to be officially "in poverty," but they can afford little more than a family that does fall below this threshold. Being poor is also not only a matter of official designation. Every individual faces a unique set of challenges, and the majority of Americans struggles to meet their financial responsibilities. Affording food is nearly impossible for those in poverty and is only slightly more attainable for those on the periphery of poverty; affording good and nutritious food is another matter altogether. Nutrition can be difficult to afford, depending on one's location and community, and many Americans, not just those officially living in poverty, have difficulty maintaining a nutritious diet.[5]

Unemployed people may face hunger, but hunger also impacts the "underemployed"—individuals unable to find full-time employment and those who can only find positions that pay less than they need to meet their financial obligations. Underemployment has increased dramatically during the COVID-19 pandemic with so many businesses closing and others operating on limited hours.[6] The unemployed have always struggled with hunger, but increasing food prices have exacerbated the problem. Over the past decade, the cost of food rose by more than 2 percent per year, while average income did not increase in concert. As a result, food has become increasingly difficult to afford, even for the fully employed. For those who are insecure in their earnings or who struggle to find enough work to meet their needs, hunger is a constant risk.

Food Security and Insecurity

While some in the United States struggle with hunger, meaning that they cannot obtain enough food from day to day, others suffer from a more nuanced condition typically called "food insecurity," which the U.S. Department of Agriculture (USDA) defines as "a household-level economic and social condition of limited or uncertain access to adequate food."[7] Families in which parents can feed their children but often go without or with less food themselves fall into the broad category of the food insecure. Families in which the food available is nutrient-poor also fall into this category. Families consuming nutrient-poor diets are more likely to suffer from obesity, heart disease, hypertension, diabetes, and other chronic diseases. People in this category may also have problems managing nutritional disease, like diabetes. Food insecurity also refers to situations in which an individual or family must choose between affording food and other essential needs.

Low-income individuals are most likely to be food insecure, but food insecurity sometimes affects those in the middle class as well, especially those insecure in their employment or who face changes in job status. Overall, a 2014 estimate found that more than 14 percent of Americans were food insecure.[8] Food insecurity is, however, much more difficult to measure because many individuals and families may experience episodes of insecurity while generally having access to food most of the time. Studies have also shown that food insecurity can have lifelong impacts on children, because inadequate nutrition is a contributor to long-term mental health problems, lower levels of educational attainment, and developmental delays. This means that food insecurity is not just an economic issue but a child welfare issue as well. Legislators have attempted to address the food insecure by expanding access to Supplemental Nutrition Assistance Program (SNAP) benefits, but this provides little remedy for those living in some areas or communities. Because food insecurity involves access to nutritious, sustaining food, and not just food in general, addressing the problem is more difficult than simply providing the ability to purchase food. Food insecurity is an issue that also involves nutritional education and raises concerns about the quality of local food markets.

A Preponderance of Issues

It is common for Americans to imagine that hunger is a matter of individual or family income, but the problem is much deeper. The entire American food industry has emphasized convenient, cheap, low-quality foods over more nutritious fare. Generations of children have been raised in environments centered around these lower-quality food options and many lack experiences with healthier diets. There are limited resources available to teach children and parents about nutrition, or to help them learn how to obtain nutritious diets. Nutritious ingredients are also more expensive Since the 1990s, healthier food has become popular, occasionally even causing a "trend" within a certain facet of the population, but the resurgence of healthy cuisine comes at a considerable cost because companies are now marketing healthier items as luxury options.

Though the issue is complex and involves many factors outside of income considerations, food insecurity and hunger are still closely linked to income insecurity and income inequality. If those at the lower end of the income spectrum were paid higher wages, it might not solve the hunger and food insecurity problem, but it would give these individuals options for family nutrition. While income is not the only factor influencing hunger in the United States, it is perhaps the most important.

Works Used

"Definitions of Food Security." *USDA*. Economic Research Service. 2020. https://www.ers.usda.gov/topics/food-nutrition-assistance/food-security-in-the-us/definitions-of-food-security.aspx.

Ewing, Jack. "United States Is the Richest Country in the World and It Has the Biggest Wealth Gap." *New York Times*. Sep 23, 2020. https://www.nytimes.com/2020/09/23/business/united-states-is-the-richest-country-in-the-world-and-it-has-the-biggest-wealth-gap.html.

"Food Insecurity: A Public Health Issue." *Public Health Reports*, vol. 131, no. 5, Sep-Oct 2016.

"Inequality: A Persisting Challenge and Its Implications." *McKinsey & Company*. Jun 26, 2019. https://www.mckinsey.com/industries/public-and-social-sector/our-insights/inequality-a-persisting-challenge-and-its-implications#s.

Lowrey, Annie. "The Underemployment Crisis." *The Atlantic*. Aug 6, 2020. https://www.theatlantic.com/ideas/archive/2020/08/underemployment-crisis/614989/.

Schaeffer, Katherine. "6 Facts about Economic Inequality in the U.S." *Pew Research*. Fact Tank. Feb 7, 2020. https://www.pewresearch.org/fact-tank/2020/02/07/6-facts-about-economic-inequality-in-the-u-s/.

Semega, Jessica, Melissa Kollar, Emily A. Shrider, and John Creamer. "Income and Poverty in the United States: 2019." *Census*. United States Census Bureau. Sep 15, 2020. https://www.census.gov/library/publications/2020/demo/p60-270.html#:~:text=The%20official%20poverty%20rate%20in,and%20Table%20B%2D5).

Tikkanen, Roosa, and Melinda K. Abrams. "U.S. Health Care from a Global Perspective, 2019: Higher Spending, Worse Outcomes?" *The Commonwealth Fund*. Jan 30, 2020. https://www.commonwealthfund.org/publications/issue-briefs/2020/jan/us-health-care-global-perspective-2019.

Notes

1. "Inequality: A Persisting Challenge and Its Implications," *McKinsey & Company*.
2. Tikkanen and Abrams, "U.S. Health Care from a Global Perspective, 2019: Higher Spending, Worse Outcomes?"
3. Ewing, "United States Is the Richest Country in the World, and It Has the Biggest Wealth Gap."
4. Schaeffer, "6 Facts about Economic Inequality in the U.S."
5. 5. Semega, Kollar, Shrider, and Creamer, "Income and Poverty in the United States: 2019."
6. Lowrey, "The Underemployment Crisis."
7. "Definitions of Food Security," *USDA*.
8. "Food Insecurity: A Public Health Issue," *Public Health Reports*.

Food Insecurity in the U.S. by the Numbers

By Christianna Silva
NPR, September 27, 2020

With COVID-19 continuing to spread, and millions of Americans still out of work, one of the nation's most urgent problems has only grown worse: hunger.

In communities across the country, the lines at food pantries are stretching longer and longer, and there's no clear end in sight. Before the pandemic, the number of families experiencing food insecurity—defined as a lack of consistent access to enough food for an active, healthy life—had been steadily falling. But now, as economic instability and a health crisis takes over, new estimates point to some of the worst rates of food insecurity in the United States in years.

"COVID has just wreaked havoc on so many things: on public health, on economic stability and obviously on food insecurity," said Luis Guardia, the president of the Food, Research and Action Center.

It's a crisis that's testing families, communities and the social safety net in ways that may have seemed unthinkable before the pandemic began. Here's a closer look at the landscape:

Nearly 1 in 4 Households Have Experienced Food Insecurity This Year

Even before the pandemic hit, some 13.7 million households, or 10.5% of all U.S. households, experienced food insecurity at some point during 2019, according to data from the U.S. Department of Agriculture. That works out to more than 35 million Americans who were either unable to acquire enough food to meet their needs, or uncertain of where their next meal might come from, last year.

For about a third of these households, access to food was so limited that their eating patterns were disrupted and food intake was reduced. The rest were able to obtain enough food to avoid completely disrupting their eating patterns, but had to cope by eating less varied diets or utilizing food assistance programs.

The coronavirus pandemic has only worsened the problem. According to one estimate by researchers at Northwestern University, food insecurity more than doubled as a result of the economic crisis brought on by the outbreak, hitting as many as 23% of households earlier this year.

Millions More Children Are Experiencing Food Insecurity

In non-pandemic times, households with children were nearly 1.5 times more likely to experience food insecurity than households without children, according to the USDA, which reported that 13.6% of households with children experienced food insecurity last year. More than 5 million children lived in these homes.

Then came the coronavirus. An analysis by the Brookings Institution conducted earlier this summer found that in late June, 27.5% of households with children were food insecure—meaning some 13.9 million children lived in a household characterized by child food insecurity. A separate analysis by researchers at Northwestern found insecurity has more than tripled among households with children to 29.5%.

School lunch programs were already struggling to meet rising demand before the pandemic. With COVID-19 now keeping children out of school, many don't have access to school lunches at all.

"The other thing that COVID has done is it's really affected kids a lot in terms of food insecurity," Guardia said. "One of the things we've noticed across the board is that households with children are more food insecure. And we believe that also has to do with school closures. So a lot of kids get their nutrition from school meals, and that's been disrupted."

Black Families Are Twice as Likely as Whites to Face Food Insecurity

The data shows that food insecurity is more likely to wreak havoc on some communities than others.

Black and Hispanic Americans are particularly disproportionately affected. According to USDA data, 19.1% of Black households and 15.6% of Hispanic households experienced food insecurity in 2019. White Americans fell below the national average, with 7.9% experiencing food insecurity.

College graduates experienced food insecurity at a rate of just 5% last year. For those without a high school degree, the rate skyrocketed to 27%. Adults who have a disability—in particular adults who have a disability and are not in the work force— also experience more than two times the rate of food insecurity as adults who do not have a disability.

19 Million Americans Live in Food Deserts

Location is another factor at play. People who live in food deserts are often more likely to experience food insecurity because food is harder to obtain where they live. About 19 million people, or roughly 6% of the population, lived in a food desert and 2.1 million households both lived in a food desert and lacked access to a vehicle in 2015, according to the USDA.

Food can also be costlier where they live. A 2010 estimate from the USDA found that groceries sold in food deserts can cost significantly more than groceries sold in suburban markets, meaning people in low-income communities impacted by food insecurity often pay more money for their food. Milk prices, for example, were about 5% more in some spots while prices for cereal were sometimes 25% higher.

The definition of food desert can change depending on where you live. In urban settings, you need to live more than a mile away from a supermarket to be considered inside a food desert. For rural areas, it's greater than 10 miles. Ru-

19% of Black households and 15.6% of Hispanic households experienced food insecurity in 2019.

ral areas are slightly more likely to be food deserts than urban areas and, according to Feeding America, and while they make up just 63% of counties in the country, they make up 87% of counties with the highest rates of food insecurity.

38 Million People Used SNAP in 2019

One in nine people in the U.S. used SNAP—the Supplemental Nutrition Assistance Program (also known as food stamps)—in 2019, according to the Center on Budget and Policy Priorities. SNAP benefits vary depending on the need of the participant, but the average SNAP benefit for each member of a household was $129 per month in fiscal year 2019.

SNAP is the largest food assistance program for low-income Americans in the nation, and because of COVID-19, demand for the program has been growing. In March, when the Families First Act passed as part of the government's emergency response to the pandemic, the maximum benefit for SNAP recipients was temporarily expanded by an estimated 40%. An analysis from the *New York Times* shows that SNAP grew by 17% from February 2020 to May 2020, three times faster than in any previous three-month period.

Yet even with that expanded food aid, the program hasn't managed to meet the nation's food security needs. Congressional Democrats have sought to increase funding for SNAP and other nutrition assistance benefits, but prospects appear uncertain.

COVID-19 Could Double the Number of People Experiencing Food Insecurity Globally

The problem is hardly unique to the U.S. According to the United Nations World Food Program, the global pandemic has the chance to double the number of people experiencing acute food insecurity, from 135 million in 2019 to 265 million in 2020.

"COVID-19 is potentially catastrophic for millions who are already hanging by a thread," the program's chief economist, Arif Husain said in a statement published this spring. "It is a hammer blow for millions more who can only eat if they earn a wage. Lockdowns and global economic recession have already decimated their nest eggs. It only takes one more shock—like COVID-19—to push them over the edge. We must collectively act now to mitigate the impact of this global catastrophe."

Print Citations

CMS: Silva, Christianna. "Food Insecurity in the U.S. by the Numbers." In *The Reference Shelf: Food Insecurity & Hunger in the United States,* edited by Micah L. Issitt, 9-12. Amenia, NY: Grey House Publishing, 2021.

MLA: Silva, Christianna. "Food Insecurity in the U.S. by the Numbers." *The Reference Shelf: Food Insecurity & Hunger in the United States,* edited by Micah L. Issitt, Grey House Publishing, 2021, pp. 9-12.

APA: Silva, C. (2021). Food insecurity in the U.S. by the numbers. In Micah L. Issitt (Ed.), *The reference shelf: Food insecurity & hunger in the United States* (pp. 9-12). Amenia, NY: Grey House Publishing.

U.S. Is a Land of Plenty, So Why Do Millions of Americans Still Go Hungry?

By Jeffrey H. Cohen and Jay L. Zagorsky
The Conversation, **March 9, 2016**

Are people in the U.S. getting enough to eat?

Unfortunately, even though the U.S. is bountiful and the world's biggest individual exporter of food, millions of Americans actually are not.

Each year the Department of Agriculture runs a nationwide survey to determine how many people go hungry. The latest figures show almost 6 percent of households–about 18 million people–are consistently not getting enough to eat. Another 8 percent–30 million people–have occasional problems feeding themselves.

Altogether, about 14 percent of U.S. households–roughly 48 million people or one in seven Americans–go hungry at some point during the year, and not because they are trying to lose weight. This number actually underestimates the problem because the survey excludes the homeless and transients, groups that almost by definition lack enough food.

Given the size of the problem, you might think it'd be a prominent issue on the campaign trail this year.

Yet none of the presidential candidates discusses this issue, even as they attend endless breakfast meetings, lunch roundtables and dinner fundraisers. It doesn't seem to be on their minds, perhaps because they are surrounded by food. A Secret Service agent assigned to protect a candidate once jokingly told one of us the most dangerous part of the job was ensuring he didn't die from overeating.

While the candidates, their staff and protectors are well-fed, the news is not as good for the rest of the country.

In other words, why do we have such a tough time ending hunger in America?

What Hunger Really Means

If you are like most people, you know what it is like to think yourself, "I'm hungry." You have probably said as much to a friend or family member.

And your hunger is real. It is a feeling of emptiness caused by a lack of food.

But being hungry in the moment–maybe you skipped breakfast or missed lunch– is not the same as hunger. Hunger is not knowing if there is a next meal, which is quite different from being temporarily hungry.

The 48 million Americans who face hunger and food insecurity are found across our nation. Yet, poverty, lack of education and state programs as well

---

Poverty and lack of access to resources are two of the key forces defining hunger in the U.S.

---

as infrastructure combine to concentrate hunger and food insecurity in the South and especially in Mississippi, Arkansas, Texas, Alabama, North Carolina and Kentucky.

According to the USDA's Economic Research Service, these food-insecure households respond to hunger and food insecurity in various ways. They eat a less varied diet, they participate in federal food assistance programs and they turn to emergency food programs including community pantries. Hungry families juggle expenses. They trade one kind of insecurity for another and forego payments for utilities in order to buy food.

Hunger has been with us for eons. Not so long ago, people suffered hunger because their crops failed, there were no animals to hunt or there was a climate catastrophe. A drought, rains or rain that arrived at the wrong time were just some of the climate events that might cause hunger.

Defining Food Security

Food security is a simple concept. People who are "food secure" have enough to eat. People who are "food insecure" do not.

Not only are the numbers large, the Department of Agriculture survey shows the percentage of households experiencing food insecurity has climbed slightly since 1995. This is shocking since the overall U.S. economy has grown roughly 60 percent over the same period, indicating economic gains alone are not improving the lives of the most vulnerable.

The survey tracks hunger each December by asking if the following statements apply:
1. "We worried whether our food would run out before we got money to buy more."
2. "The food that we bought just didn't last and we didn't have money to get more."
3. "We couldn't afford to eat balanced meals."

Using these questions and a few others, each household is classified as "food secure," "low food security" or "very low food security."

Does the U.S. Grow Enough Food?

Is the reason for such large numbers of food-insecure people that U.S. farmers are not growing enough?

Data from a special program that monitors food availability show the answer is no. For example, the U.S. produces about 200 pounds of grains like wheat, rice and oats; 250 pounds of red meat and poultry; and 200 pounds of dairy products each year for *every person in the country*. The typical hiker needs about two pounds a day when active outdoors. That means using just the three categories noted would provide enough food to satisfy the average person—and that's ignoring fruits, vegetables and everything else the U.S. grows.

Not only does the U.S. produce far more food than it needs, it could grow much more. Farmers enrolled in the Conservation Reserve Program are paid each year not to use their land. The program annually pays about US$1.7 billion a year to ensure 24 million acres are left fallow.

This means more land than the entire state of Indiana is taken out of production annually.

So Why Are People Still Going Hungry?

Given how bountiful the U.S. is, why does hunger remain a problem? Poverty and lack of access to resources are two of the key forces defining hunger in the U.S.

The link between poverty and hunger is clear. Approximately 40 percent of families living below the federally mandated poverty rate ($23,850 for a family of four in 2014) were hungry that year. Households with children, single parents and those living below the poverty line are at particular risk.

In *Child Food Insecurity: The Economic Impact on our Nation*, John Cook and Karen Jeng note that hunger and food insecurity are a health issue. Hungry children are more likely to be sick and developmentally impaired. In other words, hungry children do not live up to their potential.

Food deserts, areas that lack grocery stores, farmers' markets and access to nutritious foods, are a problem across our nation.

Recall the last time you went grocery shopping. Did you take a cab or drive yourself?

For Americans who lack cars, it is a challenge to find transportation to and from a market. Traveling home with bags of heavy, perishable goods (think of carrying a gallon of milk to and from a bus stop) is not easy. Add in the time constraints of work, child care and maintaining a home, and the challenge grows even more overwhelming.

But the challenge of hunger is not simply an urban or ethnic problem. Food deserts are a problem for rural Americans and are concentrated in the south.

Rural Americans may live hundreds of miles and many hours from a grocery store or a source of nutritious foods. In fact, more than 50 percent of all food-insecure households are found outside of metropolitan areas.

Rural and southern households pose a unique challenge. Rural homes suffer from unemployment at rates greater than their urban neighbors. Southern homes lack educational opportunities and both lack access to family-based services like affordable child care and public transportation.

Can We End Hunger in the U.S.?

Unfortunately, there is no way to prevent hunger. It is a problem that will persist. Yet we do have some ways to fight hunger and, with luck, reduce food insecurity.

Aid is a good place to start. By donating our time, money and food to local charities, we become part of the solution. But charity doesn't address the bigger challenges the hungry face.

Hunger is about health care, poverty and education. Ending hunger and food insecurity requires investing more money in these areas and enacting policies that reduce unemployment and lift wages.

We can also reduce food insecurity by improving public transportation and other infrastructure to make it easier for grocers and farmers to get nutritional food to the people who really need it.

No one should go hungry or feel insecure about their next meal in the U.S. in the 21st century. As the 2016 presidential campaign slogs on, we can be part of the solution by both giving of ourselves and asking our leaders to address this vital issue and promote food security as a sacred right for all Americans.

Print Citations

CMS: Cohen, Jeffrey H., and Jay L. Zagorsky. "U.S. Is a Land of Plenty, So Why Do Millions of Americans Still Go Hungry?" In *The Reference Shelf: Food Insecurity & Hunger in the United States,* edited by Micah L. Issitt, 13-16. Amenia, NY: Grey House Publishing, 2021.

MLA: Cohen, Jeffrey H., and Jay L. Zagorsky. "U.S. Is a Land of Plenty, So Why Do Millions of Americans Still Go Hungry?" *The Reference Shelf: Food Insecurity & Hunger in the United States,* edited by Micah L. Issitt, Grey House Publishing, 2021, pp. 13-16.

APA: Cohen, J.H., & Zagorsky, J.L. (2021). U.S. is a land of plenty, so why do millions of Americans still go hungry? In Micah L. Issitt (Ed.), *The reference shelf: Food insecurity & hunger in the United States* (pp. 13-16). Amenia, NY: Grey House Publishing.

America's Dirty Little Secret: 42 Million People Are Suffering from Hunger

By Susan Caminiti
CNBC, December 13, 2016

While families across the country gather around the dinner table during this holiday season, there is a different, far less cheery scenario playing out for millions of other Americans. They're the ones who go hungry, and for whom food—and enough of it—is a daily struggle. According to Feeding America, more than 42 million people now suffer from hunger throughout the nation.

In the midst of a recovering economy, low unemployment and nearly nonexistent inflation, the fact remains that nearly 1 in 7 Americans still goes to bed hungry each night. According to recent statistics released by the U.S. Department of Agriculture, 15.8 million U.S. households—that's 12.7 percent of the total—didn't have enough food to eat at some point last year, the latest period for which numbers are available.

That's a tick down from the 14 percent of households that didn't have adequate food (or what the USDA defines as "food insecure") in 2014, but the numbers are still higher than where they were just a decade ago. Adding to the crisis is the fact that by the end of this year, up to 1 million Americans will have lost food-stamp benefits because of changes in the law that affect eligibility.

Statistics tell the story. Last year the government doled out $74 billion in food-assistance benefits—about double the level of 2008. According to experts, hunger remains a persistent problem because millions of Americans are struggling financially as the result of the crash, and many remain unemployed. A whopping 95 million Americans are now not in the workforce, according to the November jobs report. While many are retirees, a skills gap and other factors are exacerbating the trend.

As a result, food banks, soup kitchens, churches and other emergency food providers across the country say they're seeing greater demand than ever. Perhaps more disturbing: An increasing number of working-poor families and the elderly are using these emergency services.

"There's still this idea that food banks and soup kitchens are only for the homeless, and that simply is not the case," said Margarette Purvis, president and CEO of the Food Bank for New York City, one of the largest and most active food banks in the country. "In fact, many people are pretty much relying on these resources so that they don't wind up homeless."

Among the most vulnerable in this climate are children. According to the Center on Budget and Policy Priorities, a nonpartisan research group that focuses on reducing poverty, 20 million children in the United States (nearly 1 in 4) will have received Supplemental Nutrition Assistance Program (SNAP) benefits—better known as food stamps—in 2016. With access to the food these benefits provide, experts say these children are more likely to do better in school, have better health and do better economically as adults than children that live in chronically food-insecure households.

If the economic recovery has proved anything, it's that not everyone healed in quite the same way and, in fact, millions of Americans are still struggling financially. That disparity is among the top reasons why hunger remains such an intractable problem. Ross Fraser, a spokesman for Feeding America, the national food bank network that provides food assistance to about 46 million people each year, says this uneven recovery hits the poorest Americans especially hard. "When the economy gets into trouble, you see people at the low end of the earnings spectrum be the first to suffer," he said, "and they're the last ones for whom life gets better once the economy improves."

Evidence of that scenario is nationwide. What Fraser hears over and over again from Feeding America's food banks is that while more people are working again, "those numbers disguise the fact that so many of these jobs are paying minimum wage or slightly above," he said. "Without a good income it's a real struggle to feed a family."

Indeed, a recent report by the Economic Policy Institute found that between 2000 and 2015, wages for the bottom 60 percent of male workers were flat or declined and that most of the wage gains have occurred among the highest earners. David Lee, executive director of Feeding Wisconsin, part of the Feeding America network,

Food banks, soup kitchens, churches and other emergency food providers across the country say they're seeing greater demand than ever.

puts it another way: "A good-paying job is the best antidote to hunger."

Yolanda Vega, 48, knows that all too well. The single mom lives in the East Harlem section of New York City with her 21-year-old son and 17-year-old daughter. She lost her job as a home health aide in October and is now receiving SNAP benefits. "I don't know what I would do if I didn't have food stamps," she said. "At least with this, I have money to buy food for my kids."

She gets a little more than $500 a month and manages to make it last by buying just what the family needs. Occasionally, she's able to buy fresh vegetables and fruit at a local farmer's market, where through her SNAP benefits, she gets an extra $2 for every $5 she spends. "I want to work again, but right now without these food stamps, I would not survive," she stressed.

Adding to the hunger crisis are changes taking place at the federal and state levels. Eligibility for benefits from SNAP are tightening for some groups or being slashed completely for others. Most unemployed, able-bodied adults without dependents—often referred to as ABAWDs—are limited to three months of benefits every three years, unless they are working 20 hours per week or participating in a job-training program. During the recession, when unemployment was high and job-training programs were scarce, states were able to request waivers for these work requirements, and many governors did just that.

Now, however, the USDA—the government agency that oversees food stamps programs—reports that more than 40 states will implement the time limits in at least some areas of the state, meaning that millions of people who had been eligible for food stamps no longer are. In fact, the Center on Budget and Policy Priorities estimates that at least 500,000 to 1 million Americans will have lost food-stamp benefits by the end of this year as the time limits go back into place.

Wisconsin is among the states already operating without a waiver. Lee of Feeding Wisconsin says that his state took a release from the time-limit waiver in 2014 and, as a result, 120,000 ABAWDs lost their food stamp eligibility. The official stance of the state for this move, said Lee, was that "this was the kick in the butt these people needed to get back to work."

The problem with that argument, he says, is that ABAWDs are often the most marginally employable people to begin with. "Some have physical or mental disabilities that aren't diagnosed, which makes finding and keeping a job difficult," Lee explained. Furthermore, often the training that's provided doesn't really prepare them for the jobs that are out there.

Other states go beyond the work requirements. Missouri passed a law earlier this year that reduces residents' participation in SNAP from four to five years, and in Maine, Gov. Paul LePage has threatened to overhaul or completely cease administering the food-stamp program because he believes it is a waste of public money.

States Lend a Helping Hand

But some states are going in the opposite direction. When the 2014 Farm Bill cut SNAP benefits by billions of dollars, 53,000 New York residents could have lost their food-stamp benefits. New York Gov. Andrew Cuomo was able to adjust the state's budget so that the cuts were never felt. To put that into context, the Food Bank for New York City's Purvis says if the SNAP funding cuts had gone through in New York, it would have "wiped out the amount of food it takes us all year to put out."

The governor also changed the eligibility threshold for SNAP benefits from 130 percent of the poverty line to 150 percent so that more households could get help. "These are not political moves," Purvis said. "They are changes that recognize the reality of poverty and hunger today and that more working families need help to put food on the table."

Of course, when the federal government and states make changes to hunger programs, it has a direct and hard-hitting impact on the groups that act as a safety net. It also forces them to become more creative and resourceful in how they respond. Feeding America, for example, recently rolled out a new initiative called

Meal Connect. Funded with a $1.6 million grant from Google, the online program enables smaller amounts of food to be rescued that might otherwise go to waste.

For instance, if a small butcher shop has 10 pounds of ground beef available at the end of the day, it can now log on to see which nearby food bank or pantry can use it and make arrangements for someone to pick it up. "Rescuing all these small amounts of food can really add up," said Feeding America's Fraser, who notes that the program is now in the midst of being beta-tested as an app. He estimates that since Meal Connect began earlier this year, it has rescued 200 million pounds of food.

Corporate White Knights

Feeding America is also expanding its partnerships with retailers such as Target, Safeway, Sam's Club and others to rescue food that is nearing its expiration date. As the organization improves and increases its own capacity, Fraser says it can effectively work with these large retailers and in fact has rescued nearly 1 billion pounds of food that it can distribute to its food banks.

Similarly, in the spring, the Food Bank for New York City launched a program called Green Sidewalks that brings fresh produce to neighborhoods that otherwise couldn't afford it. "We were noticing that even though we have fresh produce to distribute, some of the pantries and food banks we work with weren't taking it because they just don't have the refrigeration to store it," Purvis said. Now, with money from corporate donors, her group is able to bring that fresh produce directly to the neighborhoods and distribute it right from refrigerated trucks.

Perhaps the most heartening aspect in the fight against hunger is the commitment that no matter how great the demand, the organizations responding to this crisis manage to stay one step ahead.

Says Purvis: "The need for food can be high, but if we have an ability to hit this problem with dynamic solutions and a mixed approach, we can truly move the needle on hunger."

Print Citations

CMS: Caminiti, Susan. "America's Dirty Little Secret: 42 Million People Are Suffering from Hunger." In *The Reference Shelf: Food Insecurity & Hunger in the United States,* edited by Micah L. Issitt, 17-20. Amenia, NY: Grey House Publishing, 2021.

MLA: Caminiti, Susan. "America's Dirty Little Secret: 42 Million People Are Suffering from Hunger." *The Reference Shelf: Food Insecurity & Hunger in the United States,* edited by Micah L. Issitt, Grey House Publishing, 2021, pp. 17-20.

APA: Caminiti, S. (2021). America's dirty little secret: 42 million people are suffering from hunger. In Micah L. Issitt (Ed.), *The reference shelf: Food insecurity & hunger in the United States* (pp. 17-20). Amenia, NY: Grey House Publishing.

World Hunger Is Still Not Going Down After Three Years and Obesity Is Still Growing

United Nations, July 15, 2019

An estimated 820 million people did not have enough to eat in 2018, up from 811 million in the previous year, which is the third year of increase in a row. This underscores the immense challenge of achieving the Sustainable Development Goal of Zero Hunger by 2030, says a new edition of the annual *The State of Food Security and Nutrition in the World* report released today.

The pace of progress in halving the number of children who are stunted and in reducing the number of babies born with low birth weight is too slow, which also puts the SDG 2 nutrition targets further out of reach, according to the report.

At the same time, adding to these challenges, overweight and obesity continue to increase in all regions, particularly among school-age children and adults.

The chances of being food insecure are higher for women than men in every continent, with the largest gap in Latin America.

"Our actions to tackle these troubling trends will have to be bolder, not only in scale but also in terms of multisectoral collaboration," the heads of the United Nations' Food and Agriculture Organization (FAO), the International Fund for Agricultural Development (IFAD), the UN Children's Fund (UNICEF), the World Food Programme (WFP) and the World Health Organization (WHO) urged in their joint foreword to the report.

Hunger is increasing in many countries where economic growth is lagging, particularly in middle-income countries and those that rely heavily on international primary commodity trade. The annual UN report also found that income inequality is rising in many of the countries where hunger is on the rise, making it even more difficult for the poor, vulnerable or marginalized to cope with economic slowdowns and downturns.

"We must foster pro-poor and inclusive structural transformation focusing on people and placing communities at the centre to reduce economic vulnerabilities and set ourselves on track to ending hunger, food insecurity and all forms of malnutrition," the UN leaders said.

Slow Progress in Africa and Asia

The situation is most alarming in Africa, as the region has the highest rates of hunger in the world and which are continuing to slowly but steadily rise in almost all sub-regions. In Eastern Africa in particular, close to a third of the population (30.8 percent) is undernourished. In addition to climate and conflict, economic slowdowns and downturns are driving the rise. Since 2011, almost half the countries where rising hunger occurred due to economic slowdowns or stagnation were in Africa.

> **Over 2 billion people, mostly in low- and middle-income countries, do not have regular access to safe, nutritious and sufficient food.**

The largest number of undernourished people (more than 500 million) live in Asia, mostly in southern Asian countries. Together, Africa and Asia bear the greatest share of all forms of malnutrition, accounting for more than nine out of ten of all stunted children and over nine out of ten of all wasted children worldwide. In southern Asia and sub-Saharan Africa, one child in three is stunted.

In addition to the challenges of stunting and wasting, Asia and Africa are also home to nearly three-quarters of all overweight children worldwide, largely driven by consumption of unhealthy diets.

Going beyond Hunger

This year's report introduces a new indicator for measuring food insecurity at different levels of severity and monitoring progress towards SDG 2: the prevalence of moderate or severe food insecurity. This indicator is based on data obtained directly from people in surveys about their access to food in the last 12 months, using the Food Insecurity Experience Scale (FIES). People experiencing moderate food insecurity face uncertainties about their ability to obtain food and have had to reduce the quality and/or quantity of food they eat to get by.

The report estimates that over 2 billion people, mostly in low- and middle-income countries, do not have regular access to safe, nutritious and sufficient food. But irregular access is also a challenge for high-income countries, including 8 percent of the population in Northern America and Europe. This calls for a profound transformation of food systems to provide sustainably-produced healthy diets for a growing world population.

Key Facts and Figures

- Number of hungry people in the world in 2018: 821.6 million (or 1 in 9 people)
  - in Asia: 513.9 million
  - in Africa: 256.1million
  - in Latin America and the Caribbean: 42.5 million

- Number of moderately or severely food insecure: 2 billion (26.4%)
- Babies born with low birth weight: 20.5 million (one in seven)
- Children under 5 affected by stunting (low height-for-age): 148.9 million (21.9%)
- Children under 5 affected by wasting (low weight-for-height): 49.5 million (7.3%)
- Children under 5 who are overweight (high weight-for-height): 40 million (5.9%)
- School-age children and adolescents who are overweight: 338 million
- Adults who are obese: 672 million (13% or 1 in 8 adults)

Print Citations

CMS: "World Hunger Is Still Not Going Down After Three Years and Obesity Is Still Growing." In *The Reference Shelf: Food Insecurity & Hunger in the United States,* edited by Micah L. Issitt, 21-23. Amenia, NY: Grey House Publishing, 2021.

MLA: "World Hunger Is Still Not Going Down After Three Years and Obesity Is Still Growing." *The Reference Shelf: Food Insecurity & Hunger in the United States,* edited by Micah L. Issitt, Grey House Publishing, 2021, pp. 21-23.

APA: United Nations. (2021). World hunger is still not going down after three years and obesity is still growing. In Micah L. Issitt (Ed.), *The reference shelf: Food insecurity & hunger in the United States* (pp. 21-23). Amenia, NY: Grey House Publishing.

2
Supplementing Nutrition

School lunch programs assure at least one nutritious meal a day for many children. These Maryland students participate in a school lunch program in 2013.

Supplementing Food for Families and Children

States attempt to alleviate hunger, malnutrition, food insecurity, and child neglect through programs that provide funds to families to supplement their food budgets. These programs typically focus on the welfare of the marginalized, including children and mothers. Over the years, supplementary nutrition programs have become controversial because some Americans object to contributing to such programs indirectly through taxation and argue that they encourage individuals to avoid finding employment. Others see providing assistance for families and children as a matter of utilizing the collective resources of a society to limit the disadvantages of those at risk.

The School Lunch Dilemma

Until the late 1800s, education in many parts of the country was still voluntary and almost no states had a public education system. Instituting free, public education was perhaps the greatest progressive accomplishment in American history in terms of addressing class inequality, but it was an evolution that took well over a century and the benefits of educational reform were not evenly distributed. Predictably, the idea of using federal tax funds to pay for education met with a chilly reception from libertarian-minded individuals who tend to oppose any effort to increase taxation. Parents who obtained little education were often skeptical about the need for education, and preferred for their children to enter the workforce as soon as possible. Corporations were typically happy to have younger workers fueling their profits as well and so campaigned against the public education system. Business owners in many cases find it desirable to employ uneducated or undereducated individuals, as workers lacking in education are less likely to advance to new positions or new jobs.[1]

Nevertheless, the idea of public education has considerable pedigree. There had been a movement for free public education within the religious reforms in England prior to the establishment of the first American colony, and religious groups pioneered free education in America as well, setting up territory-run schools. Massachusetts was the standout pioneer in public education, with the Massachusetts Bay Colony passing a law in 1647 that gave the state government the power to require towns under their control to establish tax-funded schools. Many of the nation's most passionate progressives, like Thomas Jefferson and Benjamin Franklin, saw public education as a great leveler to the inequities of the class-based system that had existed in England. Thomas Jefferson famously said of education:

Educate and inform the whole mass of the people. Enable them
to see that it is their interest to preserve peace and order, and

they will preserve them. And it requires no very high degree of
education to convince them of this. They are the only sure
reliance for the preservation of our liberty...[2]

In 1900, only 34 of the 45 states had laws requiring children below the age of 14
to attend school, and there was little in the way of assistance for parents. Though
some states funded public schools, the decision to do so was up to the state. The
movement to create a federal law that would make education compulsory didn't really get started until the 1920s, when the Smith-Towner Bill was used to establish
the National Education Association. The federal government began providing states
with resources to establish and run public education systems and also made education for children under the age of 14 mandatory. Though many Americans were
dismissive of this idea and criticized the amount of funding being provided for educational systems, public education lifted countless millions out of a cycle of generational poverty and is directly responsible for the diversity of American industry and
academia today, much more so than private or religious education.[3]

The inequities that public education was supposed to address also extend into
the home and to the ability of families to provide adequate nutrition for school-age
children. This was the motivation behind the nation's first school lunch programs,
instituted in the cities of Philadelphia and Boston in the late 1800s. These were
not state-sponsored programs but the product of charitable private movements.
The Women's Educational and Industrial Union in Boston was at the center of
the movement to provide nutrition to school-aged children, while the Starr Center
Association in Philadelphia began providing meals to high school students for the
price of a single penny in 1894. Press coverage of these pioneering programs was
overwhelmingly positive, and both teachers and parents in Philadelphia and Boston
opined that providing lunches to students had resulted in positive results, both on a
physical and mental level. More and more schools began adopting similar programs,
organized through local charitable organizations.

In the early 1900s, parent-teacher organizations took a leading role in managing
school lunch programs. But in many rural areas a lack of resources made it difficult
to effectively provide for students. Along the way, the school lunch program movement became quite innovative. In some areas, parents participated in mass cooking programs to provide food for students at local schools. In some high schools,
students in home economics classes would jointly prepare lunches for students at
lower levels. The problem with allowing states and independent organizations to
manage school lunches was that the benefits were unevenly distributed. Students in
poor communities often had no school lunches, and this compounded the disadvantages already faced by families and students in these areas.[4]

The Great Depression was the turning point for federal involvement in school
lunches. Under Franklin D. Roosevelt's New Deal program, the federal government
purchased surplus crops from farmers and created a massive program to employ
thousands of cooks to prepare and serve food to students. This solution not only
provided a benefit to struggling families but also created a boom in employment
and provided funding for struggling farmers. By 1941, every state in the union had a

school meal program, but the program fell into disarray during World War II, when scarcity of resources saw the federal government abandoning the program. Activists in Congress saw this as a major loss for the nation's struggling students and parents, and bills were drafted to revive the program.

The campaign to restore school lunches took several years but resulted in the passage of the National School Lunch Act of 1946. According to the official bill:

> It is hereby declared to be the policy of Congress, as a measure of national security to safeguard the health and well-being of the nation's children and to encourage the domestic consumption of nutritious agricultural commodities and other food, by assisting the States, through grant-in-aid and other means, in providing an adequate supply of food and other facilities for the establishment, maintenance, operation and expansion of nonprofit school lunch programs.[5]

The federally funded school lunch program was popular with parents and teachers but fell victim to Ronald Reagan-era efforts to slash the federal budget. School lunches were one of the biggest cuts made by Reagan, whose administration removed $1.5 billion in part by reducing the number of poor children eligible for subsidized lunch and by shrinking portions of food. During the debate over the issue in the 1980s, the Reagan administration was heavily criticized for claiming that tomato ketchup should be considered a vegetable for the purposes of determining whether subsidized lunches met nutritional standards.

Reagan's critics accused the administration of quite literally taking food from the mouths of hungry children, but the administration countered with inaccurate claims that lunch programs were an example of bloated government waste. There was an earnest attempt to reform the system under the Obama administration, resulting in a significant increase in healthier food being provided through public schools, but the reforms met with staunch criticisms from the same groups that have long opposed school lunches, viewing them as "handouts" for the poor at the expense of taxpayers.[6]

Subsidized school lunches remain as controversial in the 2020s as in the 1980s, largely thanks to increasingly polarized views on how to spend tax revenues and a shift in conservative attitudes about the welfare of children. In many districts around the country, school lunches are paid for by families and government subsidies are meagerly distributed. Numerous articles and studies have looked at how this affects struggling families and have explored the emerging issue of "school lunch debt" that affects more families around the country. Ultimately, the students who lack access to adequate nutrition during the day are the ones who suffer. Many studies have found the adequate nutrition is essential to mental and physical functioning and have found that behavioral and performance issues in schools can often be linked to hunger and nutritional deficits. Further, because the lunches afforded to students are based on family income, the school lunch system has become an area of income stratification. For children, needing supplemental assistance has become a mark of shame and yet another instigator for bullying and conflict within school groups.

Assistance for Families

Just as concern for the welfare of children motivated the nation's first school lunch programs, concern for children was at the center of the movement to provide struggling parents and families with supplemental food budgets as well. Supplemental family nutrition assistance, often called "food stamps," and lumped into the social welfare programs derided as "welfare" by critics, has always been controversial. Many Americans have difficulty affording adequate nutrition for themselves and/or their families. Since long before the founding of the first American colonies, the wealthy elite in the monarchies of Europe used a very insidious bit of cognitive trickery to defend their position in that highly stratified society. Elites would claim that those who failed to provide for themselves were simply inferior, lacking in intelligence, work ethic, or some other quality that allowed others to succeed where they failed. This has always been a false perspective based on classist prejudice. In reality, the wealthy exert inordinate influence over the state and craft laws and policies in such a way as to make it easier for the wealthy to keep their wealth and to amass more, while making it difficult for others to achieve wealth.

In America, the wealthy elite class adopted the same propaganda that had long been used to defend the European aristocracies in the countries they left behind. They argued that their wealth was due to their superior intelligence, work ethic, or breeding, and that the "have nots" didn't deserve wealth. This same attitude had colored debates over social welfare issues from the very beginning and continues to influence those same debates in the twenty-first century. Some Americans have long believed that it is the responsibility of American citizens, as a collective, to provide help and assistance for those who struggle financially and to utilize their collective resources to elevate as many citizens as possible to sustainability. Others believe that it should not be the responsibility of the state or of taxpayers to supplement the lives of those who have failed to "make it" in society. Since the Colonial era, opponents to state taxes and later of efforts to use these taxes to establish social welfare systems, presented variations on these familiar arguments. It has frequently been argued that social welfare encourages individuals to become "lazy," or that governments are essentially paying people "not to work." It has been argued, in many subtle and often insidious ways, that poor individuals more or less deserve their plight because they must lack some substantive quality that can be found in the more affluent. Stories of Americans advancing from poverty to riches are used in a mythology of economic mobility to argue that anyone should be able to climb the economic ladder and therefore that it should not be the responsibility of productive taxpayers to supplement the lives of those who fail to advance.

The situation changed in the Great Depression. For one of the first times in American history, the unbridled and unregulated growth of the American economy became a hazard even to the wealthy. Even families that had enjoyed multiple generations of wealth fell into near poverty and many of the nation's largest industries required governmental assistance. Of course, the working class suffered more than the wealthy during the Great Depression, but the unmitigated failure of America's free market provided justification for the many groups that had long been calling for stronger governmental regulations on industry and for the establishment of social welfare programs to prevent families and individuals from falling into abject poverty.

One of the facets of the American economy that fell into turmoil was the agricultural market. With so many out of work and so many jobs and corporations closing, agricultural products were going to waste, and farmers dependent on selling those crops were falling into financial destitution. Empowered by widespread public calls for reform, the Franklin Roosevelt Administration needed to find ways to save the agricultural industry, while dealing with massive growth of the population facing hunger and unemployment. Just as the school lunch program benefitted farmers and families by utilizing underutilized crops to create school lunches, the U.S. "food stamp" program grew out of this same effort.

The initial 1939 food stamp program debuted in Rochester, New York. The program offered stamps in two different colors. Individuals could purchase "orange stamps" at an equal value, so that $1 worth of orange stamps translated into $1 worth of goods. However, food stamps could only be used for food and essentials. In addition, for each $2 of orange stamps purchased, an individual would earn $1 in blue stamps, which could be exchanged only for certain food items that were being produced at surplus levels from farmers, such as butter, eggs, prunes, flour, oranges, cornmeal, and beans. These items were subsidized by the federal government and were provided free to qualifying consumers who purchased orange stamps. Essentially, the federal government paid farmers for the surplus goods and used these to bolster the food supplies for struggling individuals and families, who could obtain half again as much food as they normally would for their money.[7]

Unsurprisingly, in the wake of the Great Depression, and with the supply shortages of World War II, the food stamp program was abandoned. However, there were many activists who called for the federal government to reinstitute a food stamp program as a permanent aid measure for needy families. Debates over this issue took place in the 1950s, but efforts were stymied in congress. President John F. Kennedy's election in 1961 saw the revival of the food stamp program through a 1961 Executive Order. In 1964, President Lyndon Johnson asked congress to pass a law making the food stamp program permanent, and this bill succeeded in passing through Congress, becoming the Food Stamp Act. Under this act states were required to develop eligibility standards, individuals were required to purchase food stamps related to their normal food expenditures, but would receive a higher number of stamps based on the estimated amount needed to supply a nutritionally adequate diet. The revived food stamp program also enabled individuals to purchase other household items, like soaps and cleaners, and created a joint system of federal and state administration.[8]

By 1981 a record 22.4 million people were participating in the food stamp program, but the incoming Reagan Administration would change things. Just as the Reagan Administration greatly cut funding for, and so diminished the quality of, school lunches, Reagan bureaucrats also cut the budget by reducing federal expenditures on the food stamp program. Many individuals who were previously eligible were cut out of the program and, as a result, hunger increased markedly. By the late 1980s, America had a severe hunger and malnutrition problem. Adding to this was that Reagan Era policies reduced income for the working class, resulted in climbing unemployment levels, and reduced funding for job training, outreach, and assistance programs. Overall, it was an extremely dangerous time to be poor in the United States, with fewer avenues for recovery and an administration openly hostile towards providing assistance for the needy.

The Clinton administration reinstituted funding for some aspects of the food stamp program and the program was updated again under George W. Bush, who shifted the nation towards a digital credit system, known as the electronic benefit transfer (EBT) program. This was the result of the Hunger Prevention Act of 1988, which called for efficiency updates. While the program regained some of its former strength under Clinton, the George W. Bush administration again proved compara- tively hostile to spending on social assistance programs. The Bush administration placed new limits on eligibility that cut millions more out of food stamp programs, set limits for the availability of food stamps for shelters and group homes. However, the administration changed direction on the issue in order to help save the ailing agricultural industry. The 2002 Farm Security and Rural Investment Act, like earlier food stamp programs, used federal funds to help farmers by funding the distribution of surplus farm goods and decreased eligibility requirements, enabling more needy individuals and families to enroll in the food stamp program.

The most recent changes to food stamp programs were enacted under the Obama Administration. The Obama Administration instituted a series of changes, includ- ing increasing allotments for state programs, early in his first term in office. It was in 2008 that paper food stamps were finally eliminated, and the program was renamed the Supplemental Nutrition Assistance Program (SNAP). Overall, the eight years of the Obama Era was marked by an expansion of the SNAP program, especially dur- ing the first four years, while the Obama Administration was faced with expanding unemployment and hunger due to the Great Recession. When Republicans gained control of the legislature, GOP legislators made efforts to limit spending on the program. The Agricultural Act of 2014 introduced a variety of measures meant to eliminate fraud and exploitation of the system, especially be retailers. The Obama Administration also funded a number of new pilot programs designed to research new ways of implementing assistance and of promoting nutrition standards among the population.[9]

The Trump Administration was typically conservative in its approach to SNAP benefits. The administration embraced proposals to limit or eliminate some as- pects of the SNAP program and, quite controversially, the Trump Administration tried to introduce changes to the program that would have eliminated benefits for more than 700,000 Americans in the midst of a pandemic that had dramatically increased unemployment and poverty rates around the country. The Administration later dropped proposed changes when public opinion polls rapidly indicated that the changes would likely be extremely unpopular.[10]

As of 2021, the SNAP program remains highly controversial. During the Trump Administration's efforts to reduce spending on supplemental nutrition, Trump appointee Sonny Perdue of the USDA stated that the program was meant to provide "assistance through difficult times, not a way of life."[11] Some version of this position has been adopted by nearly every political critic of food stamps, arguing that providing supplemental nutrition discourages unemployed individuals from looking for work or for attempting to sustain themselves. This is a familiar and long-held argument among Republican critics of government assistance or "welfare" programs, who argue that assistance will lead to a "welfare state" in which individuals shirk work and rely on their government to take care of them. This argument is common and widespread, but has little basis in reality.

Studies have repeatedly shown that those on welfare benefits, around the world, have no demonstrable impact on increasing "laziness" or discouraging work. In contrast, in many countries supplemental assistance allows individuals to pursue education or training towards advancement beyond the simple goal of obtaining employment. For most receiving SNAP benefits or other assistance, the assistance provided might be enough to prevent them from starvation and abject poverty, but falls far short of the kind of monthly earnings that might allow a person to live a happy and comfortable life. Many other studies and opinion polls have shown that the vast majority of those accepting supplemental assistance experience anxiety and insecurity as a result of needing to rely on such programs and express a clear desire to end their reliance on assistance. Most notably, studies have shown that the primary beneficiaries of supplemental programs are the children in struggling families. Children in families that receive assistance have higher rates of educational attainment, higher incomes as adults, and overall better outcomes than children from poor families not receiving supplemental assistance. When it comes to nutrition, given the overwhelming evidence suggesting that nutrition is connected to better lifetime functioning and metal capabilities, supplementing nutrition can easily make a lifelong difference in the lives of America's next generation of workers and potentially leaders.[12]

In 2021, the SNAP program still faces widespread criticism and controversy but, as America enters a new age defined, to some degree, by the deadly pandemic that swept through the world in 2020, the fight over SNAP and other welfare benefits has never been more important or impactful. As legislators struggled to decide the future of these programs, they are therefore guided by the financial turbulence of the pandemic and the way that this world-changing pandemic might impact the current generation and future generations.

Works Used

Avey, Tori. "The History of School Lunch." *PBS*. The History Kitchen. Sep 3, 2015. https://www.pbs.org/food/the-history-kitchen/history-school-lunch/.

Bartfeld, Judith, Gundersen, Craig, Smeeding, Timothy, and James P. Ziliak. *SNAP Matters: How Food Stamps Affect Health and Well-Being*. Stanford, CA: Stanford University Press, 2016.

Coffman, Steve. *Words of the Founding Fathers: Selected Quotations of Franklin,*

Washington, Adams, Jefferson, Madison, and Hamilton, with Sources. Jefferson, NC: McFarland & Company, Inc., 2012.

Fadulu, Lola. "Trump Backs Off Tougher Food Stamp Work Rules for Now." *New York Times*. Apr 10, 2020. https://www.nytimes.com/2020/04/10/us/politics/trump-food-stamps-delay.html.

Gershon, Livia. "Where American Public Schools Came From." *Jstor Daily*. Sep 1, 2016. https://daily.jstor.org/where-american-public-schools-came-from/.

Klein, Christopher. "How Did Food Stamps Begin?" *History*. Aug 27, 2019. https://www.history.com/news/food-stamps-great-depression.

"PART 210—National School Lunch Program." *USDA*. Food and Nutrition Service. 2021. https://www.fns.usda.gov/part-210%E2%80%94national-school-lunch-program.

Picchi, Aimee. "Trump Administration Still Wants to Cut Food Stamps." *CBS News*. May 15, 2020. https://www.cbsnews.com/news/food-stamps-record-trump-fights-usda/.

Rude, Emelyn. "An Abbreviated History of School Lunch in America." *Time*. Sep 19, 2016. https://time.com/4496771/school-lunch-history/.

"A Short History of SNAP." *USDA*. U.S. Department of Agriculture. Food and Nutrition Service. 2021. https://www.fns.usda.gov/snap/short-history-snap#early%201980s.

Thompson, Derek. "Busting the Myth of 'Welfare Makes People Lazy.'" *The Atlantic*. Mar 8, 2018. https://www.theatlantic.com/business/archive/2018/03/welfare-childhood/555119/.

Tyack, David. *School: The Story of American Public Education*. Boston: Beacon Press, 2001.

Notes

1. Tyack, *School: The Story of American Public Education*.
2. Coffman, *Words of the Founding Fathers: Selected Quotations of Franklin, Washington, Adams, Jefferson, Madison, and Hamilton*, p. 125.
3. Gershon, "Where American Public Schools Came From."
4. Avey, "The History of School Lunch."
5. "PART 210—National School Lunch Program," *USDA*.
6. Rude, "An Abbreviated History of School Lunches in America."
7. Klein, "How Did Food Stamps Begin?"
8. Bartfeld, Gunderson, Smeeding, and Ziliak, *SNAP Matters: How Food Stamps Affect Health and Well-Being*.
9. "A Short History of SNAP," *USDA*.
10. Fadulu, "Trump Backs Off Tougher Food Stamp Work Rules for Now."
11. Picci, "Trump Administration Still Wants to Cut Food Stamps."
12. Thompson, "Busting the Myth of 'Welfare Makes People Lazy.'"

Trump Fights in Court to Block Pandemic Food Aid for Lowest-Income Americans

By Helena Bottemiller Evich
Politico, October 26, 2020

The Trump administration is fighting in federal court to block states from giving billions of dollars in emergency food stamps to the lowest-income Americans during the coronavirus crisis.

Residents of Pennsylvania and California have sued President Donald Trump's Agriculture Department over a policy that has kept roughly 40 percent of households who rely on the Supplemental Nutrition Assistance Program from receiving any emergency benefits during the pandemic. After being ordered by a federal judge last week to proceed with the payments in the Pennsylvania case, the department is continuing to appeal.

The Agriculture Department says that it's simply following the law. A spokesperson noted that a California court recently sided with USDA on a procedural matter.

Critics say the Trump administration is trying to return to its pre-Covid mission of shrinking safety net programs, even as economists warn more help is needed for businesses and millions of households that are newly unemployed, behind on rent and struggling to buy food.

"It's almost like they're singing that old song 'Wishin' and Hopin','" because they're not dealing with reality," said Ellen Vollinger, legal director at the Food Research & Action Center, of USDA.

The USDA's policy has already kept roughly $480 million in nutrition assistance out of just Pennsylvania, a state that's suffered a particularly high unemployment rate and also is a must-win for Trump in his bid for reelection, according to a *Politico* analysis of court filings.

The legal dispute centers on how USDA has interpreted language in the nearly $200 billion Families First Coronavirus Response Act, one of the big aid packages Congress passed in March.

The law requires USDA to grant state requests to distribute emergency allotments of SNAP as long as both the federal government and the state are under an emergency declaration due to Covid-19. But there's disagreement about how to implement the requirement.

The law says the emergency payment can't be higher than existing maximum benefit levels for SNAP, thresholds that are set by the size and income level of a

---

household. USDA has taken this to mean that households already receiving the maximum benefit level each month before the pandemic—because they have little to no household income—are not eligible for any emergency payments.

Instead of giving all SNAP households emergency payments, USDA decided to bring all households up to the maximum payment levels. For a family of three, the maximum is $535 per month, which comes out to about $2 per meal per person.

"USDA's position is consistent with congressional intent and the language Congress actually passed," a department spokesperson said in an email.

One low-income individual who previously might have been getting $20 per month in SNAP benefits could be getting nearly 10 times that under USDA's policy, while another low-income person who typically gets $204 per month has seen no increase whatsoever.

"It's cruel that USDA interpreted it in such an inequitable way," said Kathy Fisher, policy director at the Coalition Against Hunger in Philadelphia.

Anti-hunger advocates say Congress clearly intended for all SNAP recipients to receive emergency allotments and that the maximums only apply to the emergency benefit, not the total benefits for a given month.

Any household that qualifies for SNAP is already barely making ends meet and is particularly at risk during an abrupt recession, advocates say. In Pennsylvania, for example, the gross income limit for a family of three to qualify for SNAP is just over $2,300 per month, or roughly $28,000 per year. A full-time minimum wage worker in the state could earn as little as $7.25 an hour, or about $15,080 per year.

> **Any household that qualifies for SNAP is already barely making ends meet and is particularly at risk during an abrupt recession.**

The USDA did allow states to boost assistance for millions of households whose incomes were high enough that they weren't already receiving the maximum payment. That increased the benefits USDA pays out each month by 40 percent, or roughly $2 billion.

"These are unprecedented times for American families who are facing joblessness and hunger," Agriculture Secretary Perdue said in a statement when USDA touted its benefits increases over the summer, adding: "Ensuring all households receive the maximum allowable SNAP benefit is an important part of President Trump's whole of America response to the coronavirus."

USDA also later announced it would bump up the maximum benefit levels by 5 percent in response to rising food costs.

While the increases were welcomed, even by the administration's critics, anti-hunger advocates have argued the department should never have left off extremely low or no-income households during the crisis.

The legal fight over emergency benefits extends back to May when plaintiffs in California filed a class action lawsuit against USDA alleging the department was violating the law for excluding some 40 percent of SNAP recipients from the emergency payments.

The state of California is currently doling out some $250 million in emergency aid per month, according to court filings. Over the summer, a federal judge in the Northern District sided with USDA and did not order a preliminary injunction. The litigation is ongoing.

In July, Community Legal Services of Philadelphia and law firm Morgan Lewis filed a similar class-action lawsuit against the department on behalf of Pennsylvanians who did not have access to increased food assistance during the pandemic because of USDA's interpretation of the law.

Last month, U.S. District Judge John Milton Younge of the Eastern District of Pennsylvania issued a preliminary injunction that blocked USDA from continuing to rely on its interpretation of the law, finding that it ran counter to Congress' intent.

USDA has repeatedly asked the court to set aside the injunction. A federal judge in Philadelphia last week issued a decision accusing USDA of essentially flouting its injunction order—calling it an act of "egregious disobedience."

The next day, the department said it would issue the additional emergency payments in Pennsylvania for the month of October, which meant recipients there would be getting an extra $59 million.

The fight over food stamps, which is heating up in the final days of the presidential election, comes as House Speaker Nancy Pelosi and Treasury Secretary Steven Mnuchin have failed to come to an agreement in time to pass another aid package before November 3.

But the administration is not giving up its fight against the additional aid for millions of households, even in a battleground state just days ahead of an election. Attorneys for USDA last week appealed to the Third Circuit and warned that if they are able to vacate the earlier injunction, the department will make the Keystone State pay the aid back.

"This reimbursement would not come from individual SNAP households," the filing noted.

A spokesperson for USDA said if the plaintiffs are successful it would "exhaust the funds appropriated by Congress for these additional COVID benefits and result in a SNAP benefit cut for every SNAP beneficiary nationwide." Judge Younge recently called this threat "a straw man argument resting on a dubious premise." SNAP benefits have never been rationed due to a lack of resources and Congress has a long history of fully funding the program regardless of which party is in control.

There is a significant amount of money on the line, both at the individual low-income household level as well as the macro-level. Economists consider SNAP benefits one of the quickest ways to infuse money into local economies because virtually all of the benefits are spent within a month of being issued.

Agriculture Department economists have estimated that every $1 spent on nutrition assistance during a downturn, there's about $1.50 of economic activity that results.

In Pennsylvania, state officials have outlined a plan for getting emergency allotments to households that haven't previously been eligible. Under the plan, a four-person household would receive an additional allotment of $340 each month.

Groups in Pennsylvania are also seeking back payments going all the way to March, a request worth nearly half a billion dollars that would be spread across hundreds of thousands of low-income households. The court has not yet decided whether retroactive payments are warranted.

"In the meantime," said Vollinger, an anti-hunger advocate at FRAC. "People are not getting the help that they need."

Print Citations

CMS: Bottemiller Evich, Helena. "Trump Fights in Court to Block Pandemic Food Aid for Lowest-Income Americans." In *The Reference Shelf: Food Insecurity & Hunger in the United States,* edited by Micah L. Issitt, 35-38. Amenia, NY: Grey House Publishing, 2021.

MLA: Bottemiller Evich, Helena. "Trump Fights in Court to Block Pandemic Food Aid for Lowest-Income Americans." *The Reference Shelf: Food Insecurity & Hunger in the United States,* edited by Micah L. Issitt, Grey House Publishing, 2021, pp. 35-38.

APA: Bottemiller Evich, H. (2021). Trump fights in court to block pandemic food aid for lowest-income Americans. In Micah L. Issitt (Ed.), *The reference shelf: Food insecurity & hunger in the United States* (pp. 35-38). Amenia, NY: Grey House Publishing.

Making SNAP Healthier with Food Incentives and Disincentives Could Improve Health and Save Costs

By Dariush Mozaffarian
Tufts University, October 2, 2018

BOSTON (Oct. 2, 2018, 2:00 p.m. ET)—Poor eating is a major cause of illness, especially from cardiometabolic conditions such as heart disease, type 2 diabetes, and obesity. These diseases generate large economic burdens for both government and private insurance programs. For individuals and their families, additional burdens come in the form of personal illness, out-of-pocket costs, reduced quality of life, and a shortened lifespan. These diet-related diseases and costs disproportionately affect low-income families in the United States.

A new Food-PRICE study from researchers at the Friedman School of Nutrition Science and Policy at Tufts University and the Harvard T.H. Chan School of Public Health modeled the health effects and cost-effectiveness of three policy interventions to incentivize healthier eating in the Supplemental Nutrition Assistance Program (SNAP).

SNAP is the foremost U.S. program providing $70 billion each year for low-wage working families, low-income seniors, and people with disabilities to purchase food. SNAP is reauthorized every five years as part of the omnibus Farm Bill, with the 2018 Farm Bill currently being crafted by Congress. SNAP currently includes relatively few incentives, disincentives, or restrictions to encourage healthier eating.

The study, published today in PLOS Medicine, estimated that $6.77 billion to $41.93 billion could be saved in healthcare costs over the model cohort's lifetime by incorporating specific food incentives, restrictions, and/or disincentives to improve food choices in SNAP. At the same time, up to 940,000 cardiovascular events and 146,600 diabetes cases could be prevented.

The three evaluated incentive/disincentive scenarios were:

- A 30 percent subsidy for fruits and vegetables (F&V), similar to the USDA FINI program currently available for some SNAP participants in certain states.

- A 30 percent F&V subsidy plus removal of sugar-sweetened beverages (SSBs) from the list of eligible purchases using SNAP funds.

- A broader incentive/disincentive program including a 30 percent subsidy

---

for F&V, nuts, whole grains, fish, and plant-based oils and a 30 percent disincentive for SSBs, junk food, and processed meats. This program, termed "SNAP-plus" by the researchers, incentivizes healthier intakes across a broader range of foods while preserving participant choice (i.e., not restricting any items from eligibility).

The impact on health outcomes, healthcare costs, and cost-effectiveness were evaluated over different time periods: 5 years, 10 years, 20 years, and lifetime. The research team estimated that, over the cohort's lifetime, the F&V incentive could prevent 303,900 cardiovascular events, add 649,400 quality-adjusted life-years (QALYs), and save $6.77 billion in healthcare costs. Adding a SSB restriction increased the benefits to 797,900 fewer cardiovascular events, 2.11 million QALYs gained, and $39.16 billion in healthcare savings.

The SNAP-plus incentive yielded the greatest corresponding gains:

- 940,000 fewer cardiovascular events;

- 2.47 million added QALYs; and

- $41.93 billion healthcare savings.

Cost-effectiveness of each scenario was evaluated from a societal perspective (accounting for costs of implementing the program and healthcare costs) and from a government affordability perspective (further adding the direct costs of the food incentives or disincentives for everyone on SNAP, including children).

From a societal perspective, all three interventions were cost-saving, leading to societal savings of $6.77 billion, $39.16 billion, and $41.93 billion over the cohort's lifetime.

From a government affordability perspective, the incentive for fruits and vegetables showed marginal cost-effectiveness at five years but was cost-effective over a lifetime (i.e., with a cost lower than the conventional healthcare threshold of $150,000 per QALY gained). Adding the SSB restriction was cost-effective at 10 years, 20 years and lifetime.

In comparison, SNAP-plus was not only cost-effective but actually cost-saving—i.e., the government gained more dollars than it spent—with net cost-savings of $10.16 billion at five years and $63.33 billion over lifetime.

To evaluate the effects of the three incentive/disincentive protocols, the research team used a validated micro-simulation model (CVD Predict) to generate a sample representative of the U.S. adult SNAP population. The data included observations from the three most recent National Health and Nutrition Examination Surveys (NHANES 2009-2014), as well as data from national surveys, published sources, and meta-analyses that included demographics, food prices, diet-disease costs, policy costs and healthcare costs.

The research team constructed a data-driven simulation for the three incentive/disincentive policy interventions. Their analysis examined effects of such interventions on the number of cardiovascular events, QALYs, program costs, healthcare savings, and cost-effectiveness for the three scenarios, compared to the outcomes under the current SNAP program.

"Systems level changes are often the most efficient and cost-effective way to gain health and reduce healthcare costs. Our findings suggest that modest incentives for fruits and vegetables could dramatically reduce the burden of disease for individuals and the healthcare costs for businesses and the government," said co-senior author Thomas Gaziano, M.D., M.Sc., who was also corresponding author on the CVD Predict modeling study. He is an assistant professor in the department of health policy and management at Harvard T.H. Chan School of Public Health and director of the global cardiovascular health policy and prevention unit at Brigham and Women's Hospital.

"About one in seven Americans participate in SNAP, a crucial and effective program to reduce hunger. Our results suggest that SNAP can also be a powerful lever to improve nutrition, reduce major diseases, and lower healthcare spending," said corresponding and co-first author Dariush Mozaffarian, M.D., Dr.P.H., dean of the Friedman School of Nutrition Science and Policy at Tufts. "SNAP-plus, the combined food incentive/disincentive, showed the largest overall gains in health and cost-savings. Such a program could be implemented now using new technologies similar to those enjoyed in a growing number of U.S. worksite wellness and insurance programs."

The study is from the Food Policy Review and Intervention Cost-Effectiveness (Food-PRICE) research initiative, a collaboration of researchers identifying nutrition changes that could have the greatest impact on improving health outcomes in the United States. The Food-PRICE initiative began in 2015 and has resulted in approximately 30 studies, assessing the American diet, food policies, and the effects of possible taxes and subsidies. The initiative's landmark paper, published in JAMA in 2017, determined that nearly half of deaths from cardiometabolic disease could be linked to over-consumption of unhealthy foods and under-consumption of healthier foods.

Junxiu Liu, Ph.D. postdoctoral scholar is co-first author and Renata Micha, R.D., Ph.D., is co-senior author. Both are at the Friedman School. Additional authors are Yue Huang, M.S., Yujin Lee, Ph.D., and Parke Wilde, Ph.D., also all at the Friedman School; Stephen Sy, M.S. and Shafika Abrahams-Gessel, Dr.P.H, both at Harvard T.H. Chan School of Public Health;

> **From a government affordability perspective, the incentive for fruits and vegetables showed marginal cost-effectiveness at five years, but was cost-effective over a lifetime.**

Colin Rehm, Ph.D., at Montefiore Medical Center; and Thiago de Souza Veiga Jardim, M.D., Ph.D., at Brigham and Women's Hospital.

This work was supported by awards from the National Institutes of Health's National Heart, Lung, and Blood Institute (R01HL130735 and R01HL115189). Additional support was provided by an American Heart Association postdoctoral fellowship. The content of this announcement is solely the responsibility of the authors and does not necessarily represent the official views of the National Institutes of Health or other funders. For conflicts of interest, please see the study.

Mozaffarian, D., Liu, J., Sy, S., Huang, Y., Rehm, C., Lee, Y., Wilde, P., Abrahams-Gessel, S., de Souza Veiga Jardim, T., Gaziano, T., and Micha, R. (2018) Cost-effectiveness of financial incentives and disincentives for improving food purchases and health through the US Supplemental Nutrition Assistance Program (SNAP): A microsimulation study. PLoS Med 15(10): e1002661. https://doi.org/10.1371/journal.pmed.1002661

Print Citations

CMS: Mozaffarian, Dariush. "Making SNAP Healthier with Food Incentives and Disincentives Could Improve Health and Save Costs." In *The Reference Shelf: Food Insecurity & Hunger in the United States,* edited by Micah L. Issitt, 39-42. Amenia, NY: Grey House Publishing, 2021.

MLA: Mozaffarian, Dariush. "Making SNAP Healthier with Food Incentives and Disincentives Could Improve Health and Save Costs." *The Reference Shelf: Food Insecurity & Hunger in the United States,* edited by Micah L. Issitt, Grey House Publishing, 2021, pp. 39-42.

APA: Mozaffarian, D. (2021). Making SNAP healthier with food incentives and disincentives could improve health and save costs. In Micah L. Issitt (Ed.), *The reference shelf: Food insecurity & hunger in the United States* (pp. 39-42). Amenia, NY: Grey House Publishing.

Why Are More Schools Going After Families for Lunch Debt?

By Emily Moon
Pacific Standard, July 26, 2019

Around 40 families in a Pennsylvania school district got a threatening letter from an administrator this month: If they failed to pay off their school lunch debt of more than $10, the district said, they could lose their children.

The letter, signed by Joseph Muth, director of federal programs for the Wyoming Valley West School District, told parents that sending kids to school without lunch money was a form of neglect, and "the result may be your child being removed from your home and placed in foster care."

Since then, local officials have condemned Muth's threats. Legal experts have weighed in, saying a parent's inability to pay would be unlikely to qualify as neglect in the state. And on Wednesday, the school board apologized for the letter and reversed its initial decision not to accept donations to pay off the $22,000 in total lunch debt in the school district, *NPR* reports.

While the groundswell of outrage has brought school lunch debt back into the national spotlight, advocates say donations and apologies will not get at the root of the problem.

No one knows exactly how much school lunch debt exists across the country, because districts keep this information under wraps, according to Elyse Homel Vitale, a senior advocate with the non-profit California Food Policy Advocates, which supports policies aimed at increasing food access. What's clear is that Wyoming Valley West is not alone: A survey from the School Nutrition Association, representing 58,000 school nutrition officials, found that more than 75 percent of school districts reported lunch debt in the previous school year, and 40 percent say their debt is growing.

The United States Department of Agriculture, which runs the National School Lunch Program, has said its funds cannot be used to wipe out school meal debt, even though the federal child nutrition programs are aimed at curbing this problem in the first place: In 2018, 30 million children living in households with incomes at or below 130 percent of poverty line received free meals through the NSLP. But fewer kids are getting free lunch with every year, the Economic Research Service has found—and even more are denied meals because of administrative errors or the program's limitations.

Kids who are in households receiving benefits through the Supplemental Nutrition Assistance Program are automatically eligible for free meals, but school districts and states have to certify them first. Accord-

75 percent of school districts reported lunch debt in the previous school year, and 40 percent say their debt is growing.

ing to Food Research & Action Center analyst Crystal FitzSimons, this isn't always done correctly: Some states simply fail to enroll the 95 percent of SNAP participants required to be enrolled by the USDA. Other times, a child gets overlooked when their name is misspelled.

The consequences for such a small error can be extreme: As previous investigations from the non-profit newsroom New Food Economy have shown, families sometimes believe their child is receiving free meals, while they're actually racking up hundreds of dollars in debt—debt that districts can then go after using for-profit collection agencies. The majority of districts in SNA's 2018 survey said they notify parents directly about debt or offer some kind of assistance, but only half accept donations.

One reason for the increase in controversies like this one might be that the USDA required schools to begin collecting unpaid meal debt in 2017, according to SNA spokesperson Diane Pratt-Heavner.

There's also a wider problem with the NSLP: Its eligibility criteria uses what economists agree is an outdated measure of poverty that overlooks cost of living and other factors that cause children to be food insecure.

Many districts are already pursuing one potential solution to the problem: opting into a new provision of the program, known as community eligibility, which started in 2014. Under community eligibility, schools with a certain percentage of low-income kids qualify to provide free meals to the entire student body. This allows children who can't navigate the application process or are not eligible for free meals but are still food insecure to get free meals without the hassle of signing up. "What can happen immediately is schools who are eligible through the federal nutrition programs can serve meals universally free, so there isn't a federal definition of low-income driving whether a family has access to meals," Homel Vitale says.

"[Community eligibility] really is designed to support high-need schools," FitzSimons says. If a district has a lower percentage of low-income students, it can sometimes still opt in—but it will only be reimbursed for a certain percentage of the meals it offers. Schools can also eliminate the co-pay for kids who receive reduced-price lunch (in households 130 to 185 percent of the poverty line) and simply charge those meals to the school nutrition account.

According to FRAC's database, 4,633 school districts—serving 13.6 million children—have adopted community eligibility. But in Pennsylvania, only 959 of the 1,264 eligible schools have done so. None of the three schools listed under the Wyoming Valley West School District are participating in the community eligibility provision, or CEP: Two are not eligible, but one elementary school has more than 40 percent "identified students" (those students automatically eligible for free lunch), meaning it could adopt the program.

In some districts, administrators have determined that feeding kids for free is not worth the cost. "School are big businesses, and they have large budgets to balance," Homel Vitale says. "I would hope that doesn't get in the way of a school choosing to adopt CEP, but certainly it does sometimes."

Oregon recently passed a law to get around this problem, guaranteeing that schools will be reimbursed for 90 percent of their free meals, no matter their poverty level. California has seen adoption rise since the state required the poorest schools to provide free meals.

Legally, it's within a school's rights to reach out to families and ask them for the fees. But when a family is being threatened with foster care for a couple of unpaid meals? "[School lunch debt] shouldn't stand in the way of a student being able to learn," Homel Vitale says.

Print Citations

CMS: Moon, Emily. "Why Are More Schools Going After Families for Lunch Debt?" In *The Reference Shelf: Food Insecurity & Hunger in the United States,* edited by Micah L. Issitt, 43-45. Amenia, NY: Grey House Publishing, 2021.

MLA: Moon, Emily. "Why Are More Schools Going After Families for Lunch Debt?" *The Reference Shelf: Food Insecurity & Hunger in the United States,* edited by Micah L. Issitt, Grey House Publishing, 2021, pp. 43-45.

APA: Moon, E. (2021). Why are more schools going after families for lunch debt? In Micah L. Issitt (Ed.), *The reference shelf: Food insecurity & hunger in the United States* (pp. 43-45). Amenia, NY: Grey House Publishing.

Debt Collectors Over Kids' School Lunch Bills? It's Real

By Jessica Fu
Yes! Magazine, May 8, 2019

This article was originally published by The New Food Economy, a nonprofit newsroom covering the forces shaping how and what we eat. Read more at newfoodeconomy.org.

Candrice Jones thought she was in the clear. It was the fall of 2015, and she had just submitted the necessary paperwork to secure free lunch for her son Kyrie, a seventh-grader at Coolidge Junior High School in Granite City, Illinois. This, she believed at the time, would lift a significant economic load off her plate. Jones was working various part-time handwork jobs for a temp company, and her husband was unemployed after suffering injuries in a car accident. Previously, he'd worked in warehousing. She couldn't afford to cover the cost of a full-price, hot school meal every day—not if she wanted to pay the bills, too.

Every day, Kyrie did what school kids across the country do. He punched his student number into a keypad at the end of the lunch line, ate his food in the cafeteria with friends, and got on with the second half of his school day.

But over a year later, Jones discovered that Kyrie's free lunch application had been processed incorrectly. After she'd submitted it, the program covered Kyrie's meals for just one month. Reimbursements then dropped off for reasons the school has not made clear to Jones. Instead of getting free lunch every day, Kyrie had been racking up lunch debt—nearly $1,000 worth of it.

Generally, parents can monitor their children's lunch balances online. Coolidge Junior High, like many schools, uses a software system called Skyward to keep families updated on grades and lunch dues owed. But Jones didn't use the program because Kyrie's grades weren't logged into that particular system. He has a learning disability and participated in an individualized education program, which provides its paper evaluations by mail.

It wasn't until one of Kyrie's teachers unintentionally caught a glimpse of his lunch account balance in passing that Jones was alerted to the error. A full year had passed, and the debt—a mass of incremental charges—had accumulated into a single, daunting total.

"It's almost a thousand dollars," Jones told me by phone. She couldn't pay it off if she wanted to: "I don't even have it."

When Jones filed a second free-lunch application, the application "worked" and Kyrie's lunches were covered for the remaining months of eighth grade. As for the lingering debt, a school administrator suggested making monthly payments.

Jim Greenwald, superintendent of the Granite City School District, declined to comment on the Jones' case for this story, citing privacy guidelines. But he did point out that all students are served hot meals regardless of their ability to pay. Which isn't the same as getting free lunch. Students still remain on the hook for every lunch they eat. That's the reason why, even now, Kyrie's middle school lunch debt remains on his record and continues to cast a shadow over his academic experience.

Now a sophomore at Granite City High School, Kyrie has been barred from attending any school events hosted by the district. He wasn't permitted to attend homecoming at the start of his ninth grade year. Instead, he stayed at home and did Facetime with his friends who were at the dance. He didn't attend homecoming last fall either, and isn't expecting to attend prom when he's a senior.

Kyrie's case is unique because it stems from what seems to have been a clerical error, but it demonstrates the toll an unpaid lunch balance can take on a student and their family. It's also just one facet of America's ballooning school lunch debt problem. Schools themselves, in some cases, are struggling as they attempt to strike a balance between accommodating those who can't pay for lunch and balancing their books.

"Lunch shaming" refers to methods schools use to stigmatize students who can't afford the full price of school lunch.

There's no official estimate on the cumulative total of school lunch debt nationwide, as I've reported previously. But according to a survey of 1,500 school districts represented by the School Nutrition Association, median lunch debt rose from $2,000 to $2,500 per district between 2016 and 2018, and anecdotal stories from individual districts paint an increasingly concerning picture.

Local news outlets report on surges in unpaid debt on a regular basis, from Redmond, Oregon, to Shawnee Mission, Kansas, to name some recent examples. In December, The *Washington Post* reported that K-12 students in the D.C. area, which comprises multiple school districts, owed a collective $500,000 in unpaid lunch balances. At the end of the 2017-18 school year, Denver's school districts saw meal debt rise to $356,000 from $13,000 in 2016—more than a 2,600 percent increase.

"School districts nationwide are really feeling the squeeze … and, unfortunately, I think we're going to be hearing more about this in the coming years," said Diane Pratt-Heavner, director of media relations for the School Nutrition Association, referring to the persistence of school lunch debt. "For a lot of districts, you're looking at having to cover these costs out of the general fund. And if it's year after year, and it's an excessive amount of debt for the school district, that's impactful to core educational activities."

Had Kyrie's free lunch application been processed correctly, the school district would have been reimbursed for the cost of every meal he was served during the school year. The National School Lunch Program, which is administered by the United States Department of Agriculture's Food and Nutrition Service, subsidizes the cost of lunch for low-income families.

Students from families with incomes below 130 percent of the federal poverty threshold ($32,630 for a family of four) are eligible for free lunch. Students from families with incomes above that value but below 185 percent of the threshold ($46,435 for a family of four) qualify for reduced-price lunch. The exact reimbursement rates are determined by an array of factors, including location and area poverty levels.

According to USDA's Economic Research Service, the federal lunch program spends $13.6 billion on reimbursements annually. But funding comes with its own set of limitations. Schools are permitted to use the money toward obvious costs of running a cafeteria, like ingredients and workers, as well as indirect costs, like payroll and gas. However, they're prohibited from using it to wipe out unpaid lunch debt.

They are, however, permitted to use the funds toward contracting a for-profit collection agency to collect that debt.

That's why schools put so much pressure on families to pay outstanding balances. Some, as in Kyrie's case, prevent students from participating in school events until the debt is cleared. Others go so far as to prevent students with lunch debt from receiving their diplomas. To Jones, this exemplifies a broken school-lunch system, one that uses students' needs as collateral to leverage money from parents.

"They know your kids are going to be upset. They know your kids are going to be mad. And so they know that your kids are going to press you to get this bill paid," she told me. "I felt bad as a mother because I couldn't take care of the bill."

Though total lunch debt varies by district, most reporting on the issue credits its rise to policies that prohibit the practice of "lunch-shaming," which refers to methods schools use to stigmatize students who can't afford the full price of school lunch. Some schools literally stamp students who can't pay, others serve them cold "substitute" lunches like sandwiches instead of hot meals. The practice has come under intense scrutiny in recent years.

Shaneka Jackson's daughter, London, a first-grader in Baltimore County, Maryland, experienced lunch-shaming firsthand. Every day for over a month, Jackson said in a phone interview, London's hot lunch tray was taken away, thrown out, and replaced with a cold cheese sandwich. She said she had noticed London's eating habits changing at home but didn't realize that they were linked to her lunch experiences at school. Until one morning when London, in tears, pleaded to stay home.

"My daughter was humiliated. A couple of her friends were teasing her in school because her food kept getting thrown away," Jackson said. "She's in the first grade, she's only 6 years old. She's never had anybody not feed her."

Jackson, an army veteran and single mother of three, works full time as a bartender at a well-known restaurant chain. And she knew that London qualified for free lunch under the National School Lunch Program income guidelines. But instead of that, London was given cheese sandwiches instead of a hot lunch because her school had erroneously recorded her lunch account as having a negative balance of $1.60.

Jackson said she was incensed that her daughter had been going so long without warm meals over such a minute negative balance, and that she was never notified about it.

"The days that my child was hungry and nobody said anything? That really made me so upset, angry, I was disgusted. I couldn't believe it," she said. "I felt like less of a mom that I was unable to put two and two together with the signs that [that] was going on with my child."

In 2014, Food and Nutrition Service found that students were being lunch-shamed at 60 percent of public schools across the country. Since then, the practice has been widely criticized by parents, educators, administrators, and antihunger advocacy groups. In 2017, New Mexico became the first state to ban lunch-shaming policies. Many other states have followed suit, including Washington, Pennsylvania, and California.

Numerous news stories have suggested that an end to lunch-shaming is the driving force behind rising debt. But Keith Fiedler, director of nutrition services at Redmond School District in Oregon, thinks that's an oversimplification.

"That is a factor—there's no doubt," he said. Fiedler has worked in school nutrition services since 1991. "[H]ad it just been that alone, meal account debt would have gone up, but it probably would have just gone up to a new normal that was a manageable cost of doing business."

Fiedler said there are many nuances in school food operations that contribute to the lunch debt issue, including rising food and labor costs. He also pointed out that USDA's income guidelines for free lunch fail to accommodate for complex socioeconomic realities, such as high costs of living in many cities.

"The issue is very complex and includes a range of factors from regulatory, legislative, economic, social, financial, to pedagogical."

In the same 2014 study, the Food and Nutrition Service found that 35 percent of schools resort to "administrative actions," like prohibiting a student from attending homecoming because they've got lunch debt. Another 6 percent of schools send unpaid bills to collections agencies.

The Columbia Public School District in Missouri is one such example. It's the seventh largest district in the state, serving over 18,000 students. It also prohibits lunch-shaming. To curb its lunch debt problem, it signed a four-year contract with Hawthorn Recovery Services, a collection agency that goes after families with unpaid lunch bills. The agency retains a percentage of the sums it recoups.

When I asked Laina Fullum, director of nutrition services for the district, how much Hawthorn Recovery Services had collected, she declined to give a number. Fullum suggested this figure wouldn't be reflective of the contract's efficacy. She did say that often just receiving a letter from Hawthorn is enough to push parents to pay off debt directly to the district.

"Moving forward, our measure of success would be that our debt doesn't continue to accumulate or levels off," Fullum said. "We're just trying to survive this new financial situation … in all the national school-lunch programs across the nation."

Columbia is far from the only district that uses a collection agency to recoup student lunch debt. In December, the Cranston Public School District in Rhode Island was widely criticized for contracting with a collection agency to go after unpaid dues. In the prior school year, it had written off nearly $100,000 in debt.

In 2017, California banned schools from contracting with debt collectors entirely to collect unpaid lunch balances. But for much of the country, debt collection and lunch-shaming are the best ways schools have figured out how to mitigate lunch debt in the near term. The long game is another story.

School nutrition advocates I spoke with said that universal school lunch is the surest way to guarantee healthy meals for all students without impacting school operating budgets.

"The issue of unpaid school meal debt really does shine a light on the challenges within the school nutrition programs," said Crystal FitzSimons, director of school and out-of-school programs for the Food and Research Action Center, an antihunger nonprofit. "In an ideal world, school breakfast and school lunch would be offered at no charge to all students, and that would be the easiest way to solve school districts' challenges with unpaid school meal debt."

That's not as pie-in-the-sky as it may sound. Many low-income areas already serve lunch at no charge to students under a USDA program called Community Eligibility Provision, which was launched nationwide in 2014. Under that program, schools that serve a certain threshold of students who qualify for free or reduced-price lunches can simply bypass the logistical hurdle of collecting and submitting applications altogether.

The program has seen increasing participation since its launch. In the fall of 2017, the New York City School District—the largest in the nation—began operating under Community Eligibility Provision. Today, its millions of students eat lunch at no cost during the school year and can also access free lunches through its free summer meals program.

As of the 2016-17 school year, less than half of eligible school districts had actually adopted Community Eligibility Provision, according to Food Research and Action Center. Although it can be an effective tool for feeding students in income-strapped districts, it does come with stipulations.

First, schools aren't actually reimbursed for every meal they serve to students. Instead, each district receives reimbursements for whatever percentage of their student body qualifies for free and reduced-price lunches, multiplied by 1.6. For many schools under Community Eligibility Provision, that means swallowing some operational costs.

The Redmond School District in Oregon was previously part of the program. But Fiedler said the district eventually left it because it got too costly.

Advocates hope that the program will be adapted and improved in the future, because when it works, it works. Unlike the free and reduced-price lunch program, Community Eligibility Provision takes paperwork out of the equation for families. It also relieves school administrators of the exacting responsibility of tracking down individual families to write off debt.

"Charging some families and not charging others, and then school districts having to struggle to collect that unpaid school meal debt, is not a great situation for anyone," FitzSimons said.

Recall the Granite City School District where Kyrie goes to school. There, 17.6 percent of residents live in poverty, according to the most recent census. That's 5 percentage points higher than the national poverty rate. Within the school district, 62.2 percent of students are considered "low income," a broad term that includes children of families who receive public aid, children in foster care, and children who qualify for free and reduced-price lunches.

In the 2015-16 school year, only the district's elementary schools participated in Community Eligibility Provision. At the time, lunch debt for junior high and high schools totaled nearly $26,000. The next year, that number rose to more than $38,000. In the fall of 2017, the district expanded its participation to include junior high schools. As a result, the district's lunch debt dropped to about $12,500, and all students from kindergarten to eighth grade could eat lunch without cost or paperwork.

But it was too late for Kyrie, who had moved on to high school by then.

Print Citations

CMS: Fu, Jessica. "Debt Collectors Over Kids' School Lunch Bills? It's Real." In *The Reference Shelf: Food Insecurity & Hunger in the United States,* edited by Micah L. Issitt, 46-51. Amenia, NY: Grey House Publishing, 2021.

MLA: Fu, Jessica. "Debt Collectors Over Kids' School Lunch Bills? It's Real." *The Reference Shelf: Food Insecurity & Hunger in the United States,* edited by Micah L. Issitt, Grey House Publishing, 2021, pp. 46-51.

APA: Fu, J. (2021). Debt collectors over kids' school lunch bills? It's real. In Micah L. Issitt (Ed.), *The reference shelf: Food insecurity & hunger in the United States* (pp. 46-51). Amenia, NY: Grey House Publishing.

Schools Are Shaming Kids Who Can't Afford Lunch, but There Are Ways to Stop It

By Monica Humphries
NationSwell, August 14, 2019

Stephanie Woodard still remembers the weight of a roll of pennies in her pocket, hoping it would be enough to pay for lunch.

The professional learning specialist for Fort Bend International School District recalls sneaking into her father's bedroom and digging through his green can of spare change.

And when there wasn't enough money, she remembers being handed a saran-wrapped peanut butter and honey sandwich.

"I didn't want to eat peanut butter and honey, and I didn't want to be the one kid at the table who didn't have a real lunch," she said. "It made me feel terrible."

Woodard didn't qualify for free or reduced lunch because both of her parents had full-time jobs. But her father struggled with drug and alcohol addiction, and so there wasn't always money for lunch.

Decades later, Woodard, who was a middle school teacher from 2005 to 2010 in the same district where she grew up, noticed that schools were still participating in "lunch shaming." When students hit a negative lunch balance, typically the equivalent of a few lunches, cafeteria workers would print out the balance on a neon sheet of paper and place it on the lunch tray.

"The kids would hate to get it, and they would hate to take it home," Woodard said. "When you don't have money, every little thing is a way to draw attention to the fact that you don't have money."

In 2017, Texas Gov. Greg Abbott passed a bill with the goal of ending lunch shaming—this legislation allows for a grace period before students are served an alternative meal. But the practice of lunch shaming wasn't just happening in Texas. It was, and continues to be, a daily occurrence in school districts across the United States.

Lunch shaming disproportionately affects marginalized families and goes beyond just hurting a student's self-esteem. Missing meals hinders children's development and success, and for many low-income students, lunch might be their only meal of the day.

To address this issue, legislators are proposing bills, nonprofits are launching campaigns, and powerful individuals are speaking up to help end lunch shaming.

The Shameful Act of Lunch Shaming

Lunch shaming is a direct consequence of meal debt. If students have meal debt that's not paid off, the burden falls on the school to cover it.

Here's how meal debt happens: Schools receive federal reimbursement from the United States Department of Agriculture (USDA) for students who qualify and enroll in free or reduced lunch and breakfast. If the total income of a family of four falls below $32,630, the student qualifies for free lunch and breakfast. If it's below $46,435, the student qualifies for reduced breakfast and lunch.

For each child who qualifies for free meals, the school receives $3.41 for every one of their meals. For those who receive reduced meals, schools receive 32 cents. Students are automatically certified for free lunch and breakfast if their family receives assistance program benefits, such as Supplemental Nutrition Assistance Program (SNAP) or Temporary Assistance for Needy Families (TANF).

"That $3.41 has to pay for not only the food—which is a milk, a fruit, a vegetable, a grain and a protein with every lunch—but it also has to pay for labor, and benefits, and supplies, and electricity, and water and everything," Diane Pratt-Heavner, director of media relations for School Nutrition Association (SNA), told *NationSwell*.

But the one thing it can't pay for is meal debt. The USDA forbids schools from using that money to cover what it deems "bad" debt. The agency requires schools to attempt to collect debt for unpaid meals, but if those attempts to recoup the debt do not work, it falls on the school to pay for it.

Where might this money come from? Perhaps from sales of a la carte items sold in cafeterias, charitable organizations or from the school's general funds, said Pratt-Heavner.

But even if schools could use money from the federal government, "there's just not enough funds available to cover unpaid meal debt," Pratt-Heavner said.

No one knows how much lunch debt exists, but 75% of school districts reported having some amount of meal debt at the end of the 2016-2017 school year, according to SNA. For smaller school districts, it was less than $10, whereas other districts have reported upward of $865,000. The average amount of debt a district carried was $2,500.

> Lunch shaming disproportionately affects marginalized families and goes beyond hurting a student's self-esteem.

Schools are motivated to get that money back. So they've turned to lunch shaming practices like stamping children's hands with "I need lunch money" or making them clean tables when lunch is over. Schools have even sent debt collectors after families.

"In our view, school meals are just as important to learning as textbooks and pencils and paper."—Diane Pratt-Heavner, director of media relations for School Nutrition Association.

In 2010, when Congress passed the Healthy Hunger-Free Kids Act, it required the USDA to look at unpaid school meal debt. As a result, the USDA required school districts to create a written policy addressing debt. But that was where the guidelines ended, and as a result, policy varies greatly among districts.

Some policies were two sentences, while others were two pages.

"There were no minimum standards there," Crystal FitzSimons, the director of school and out-of-school time programs at the Food & Research Action Center (FRAC) said. "There were no protections for kids. Nothing."

A student can't learn if he or she is hungry.

According to school advocates, like FRAC, creating a consistent approach across all school districts is key to ending the practice of lunch shaming. So some government officials are leading the way through legislation.

In 2017, legislators in New Mexico passed an anti-lunch-shaming bill and became the first state to outright ban lunch shaming. Since then, other states, like West Virginia and California, have followed suit.

But some politicians want to take that ban nationwide.

In June, Minnesota Rep. Ilhan Omar and Sen. Tina Smith introduced the No Shame at School Act in Congress, which would set a standard for what schools can and can't do to a student who carries lunch debt. This follows New Mexico Sen. Tom Udall and New Mexico Rep. Deb Haaland's Anti-Lunch Shaming Act of 2019.

Omar's bill is the more comprehensive of the two, and if it were to pass, schools would be required to communicate directly with the parents about any lunch debt.

That means schools would no longer be allowed to publicly identify students, whether that be stamping their hands or making them wear a wristband. It would also prohibit schools from stigmatizing students, by preventing them from attending school dances, for example. Finally, schools would not be permitted to force the student to perform chores or activities that the general student body isn't required to do.

The bill would also require schools to attempt to certify children with debt and allow schools to receive retroactive reimbursement for the meals for up to 90 days. Finally, it would ban debt collectors from seeking overdue fees.

"Hunger and debt are a national problem," Omar told ABC. "So, what this bill does is simple, it prohibits the punishment and shaming of children who are unable to pay school meal fees."

If the bill doesn't pass, the fight isn't over. FRAC, a leading anti-hunger nonprofit in support of the bill, cites best practices for schools to approach lunch debt and avoid lunch shaming. Through strategic communication about free and reduced lunch, and by using new technology, like text alerts or automated refill programs, the goal is to get the children fed without financially burdening schools.

FitzSimons said schools should never let students be the messenger. Instead, schools need to communicate directly with parents and guardians. "We recommend not having any practices that overtly identify or stigmatize these kids whose families are carrying unpaid school meal debt," she told *NationSwell*. "So that's the first and most important thing."

Other communities are working on the problem at the district and individual school levels. Dozens of GoFundMe pages have been launched to collect money, and a few nonprofits have been created as a direct response to lunch debt.

However, ending school lunch shaming doesn't end school lunch debt. A few school districts have seen ballooning debt following bans on lunch shaming. For example, when Denver Public Schools announced it would no longer deny hot meals to students, debt rose from $13,000 to $356,000 in a year, partly because families were no longer incentivized to fill out forms for free and reduced lunch or pay for lunch. Thus policy changes are still needed to ensure schools can feed their students without racking up debt.

Healthy, Happy Children

Lunch-shaming bans are steps in the right direction. But it doesn't address the root cause: Not every student can afford lunch.

"It's not like it's just one thing that is driving the debt, and it's not just one kind of parent," FitzSimons said.

There are many factors that can lead to a family acquiring lunch debt. For example, immigrant families might fear filling out the federal form, even though non-U.S. students qualify for free and reduced lunch. Or families may need some financial support but not technically qualify for free or reduced lunch. The application process can be lengthy and cumbersome, so families may fill out the form incorrectly, and unknowingly rack up meal debt. Some families are uncomfortable asking for assistance, while other families might not know they qualify for it.

Students going into debt can often be a flag that something more is happening in the household, FitzSimons said. It's important schools recognize and quickly address why a student might be accruing debt. FRAC encourages schools to reach out and see if the families are eligible for free or reduced lunch when something like this happens.

Pratt-Heavner's team at SNA urges Congress to adopt a universal free school meal policy. This policy would eliminate both meal debt and lunch shaming by providing every child with free breakfast and lunch. A universal meal policy has been supported by multiple presidential candidates and has gained momentum, buoyed by recent media coverage.

The only thing currently like a universal free lunch program is the federal Community Eligibility Provision (CEP). This program offers free breakfast and lunch to all students in the nation's highest poverty school districts. If 40% of students in a district automatically receive free meals, the schools can participate in the program. This makes sure every student eats, while also eliminating paperwork and the potential for school meal debt.

Under CEP, schools are reimbursed using a formula based on the percentage of students who automatically qualify for free school meals, i.e., families who participate in programs like SNAP or Medicaid, for example.

Schools where that percentage is 62.5% or higher, the government reimburses the school for *all* meals consumed by any student at that school. If the percentage of students who would automatically be enrolled with free lunch is between 40% and

62.4%, the schools are fully reimbursed for that percentage and partially reimbursed for the meals of students who do not qualify. This will cost the district some money, FitzSimons said, but the district will also save money and time by eliminating paperwork.

"That not only eliminates the unpaid meal debt issue, it also eliminates any stigma with participating in free meals," Pratt-Heavner said.

Schools hovering slightly above the 40% are more hesitant to participate because the composition of their student bodies could change. "If you've been participating in CEP and providing these free meals for families for a few years, and then suddenly you lose your eligibility, then you're going to have some disappointed parents on your hands," Pratt-Heavner said.

Schools are even more hesitant to enroll after Trump's proposal to cut access to food stamps. This cut would change the number of students who automatically qualify for free lunch, which in turn would impact the school's CEP eligibility.

However, for schools that hit the 62.5% mark, CEP has been a success. "It is definitely the best solution. It puts everybody on a level playing field, it makes sure that all kids in the school have the nutrition they need to learn and focus and concentrate," FitzSimons said. School districts in cities like Detroit, Baltimore and New York have enrolled in the program, and report higher school attendance rates with happier and better-focused students.

Students need to be fed nutritious meals, Pratt-Heavner said. "In our view, school meals are just as important to learning as textbooks and pencils and paper."

Print Citations

CMS: Humphries, Monica. "Schools Are Shaming Kids Who Can't Afford Lunch, but There Are Ways to Stop It." In *The Reference Shelf: Food Insecurity & Hunger in the United States,* edited by Micah L. Issitt, 52-56. Amenia, NY: Grey House Publishing, 2021.

MLA: Humphries, Monica. "Schools Are Shaming Kids Who Can't Afford Lunch, but There Are Ways to Stop It." *The Reference Shelf: Food Insecurity & Hunger in the United States,* edited by Micah L. Issitt, Grey House Publishing, 2021, pp. 52-56.

APA: Humphries, M. (2021). Schools are shaming kids who can't afford lunch, but there are ways to stop it. In Micah L. Issitt (Ed.), *The reference shelf: Food insecurity & hunger in the United States* (pp. 52-56). Amenia, NY: Grey House Publishing.

3
Finding Food

By Elvis Batiz via Wikimedia.

Food aisle in small urban market with less nutritious dried/processed foods.

Food Deserts and the Search for Nutrition

Food deserts are areas in which people lack easy access to food or to nutritious and affordable food. These areas of low availability can be contrasted with the incidence of a food oasis, where food is more plentiful and affordable. The development of food deserts is multifaceted, involving many factors including income and wage stagnation, the influence of corporations, and municipal planning. Researchers have found substantive links between food deserts and numerous other public welfare problems, such as obesity and malnutrition-related disease.

What Is a Food Desert?

A food desert is, simply, an area in which it is difficult to obtain food or nutritious food. Food deserts can appear in any area. Some are urban, others suburban, and others are rural. The food desert can be contrasted with the "food oasis," which is an area in which residents have access to a variety of food or to nutritious and affordable food. Food deserts often form in areas near where major chains have been established or where demographic changes, changes in the cost of living, or changes in the cost of real estate have resulted in limiting local food options. Food deserts can also be created when new housing developments are established in areas lacking access to sufficient food resources.

Officially, the definition of a food desert differs depending on whether the area in question is urban or rural. For urban areas, the U.S. Department of Agriculture (USDA) defines a food desert as a region in which at least a third of the population lives more than a mile from a supermarket. A rural area is considered a food desert if the nearest grocery store is at least ten miles away from the population. Utilizing this definition, around 19 million people in America live in a food desert. Poorer neighborhoods are less likely to have grocery stores within the 1- to 10-mile radius and so are more likely to be classed as food deserts.[1]

Why Are Food Deserts a Problem?

The economic challenges facing working class Americans are well known and have been thoroughly explored by researchers in a variety of fields. One of the economic challenges that Americans face is in maintaining a healthy, functional diet and those in food deserts experience additional difficulties in doing so in comparison to those living in areas with convenience access to nutritious food.

Residents who live in food deserts face additional logistical or financial difficulties in trying to feed themselves or their families, and this can contribute to a variety of other problems facing low income families and individuals. Research has shown, for instance, that students who lack access to adequate food or nutrition have higher levels of difficulty with concentration and other cognitive processes and this can contribute to educational problems. In 2014, researcher Seth Frndak found a correlation between living in a food desert and poor academic achievement. Frndak, of the University of New York, Buffalo, analyzed 200 urban and suburban school districts and located food deserts within this area. Then he correlated these with fourth grade test scores and health data on students. He concluded that individuals living in areas where nutritious, affordable food was more difficult to obtain had increased difficulty with achievement measures in school.[2]

For people of all ages, living in a food desert can be a significant source of stress and can lead to anxiety and contribute to other mental health issues.[3] A lack of access to affordable, nutritious food can contribute to a number of physiological conditions as well and may have severe impact on the health of individuals with existing medical conditions. Elderly individuals living on fixed incomes or struggling with physical and mental health challenges may be especially vulnerable when living in a food desert and may experience additional difficulties in trying to compensate for the lack of local foods available in their area. A 2018 study found that the criteria used to define food deserts by organizations like the USDA may in fact underestimate the impact of the food desert phenomenon with regard to the aging and elderly populations. For older individuals, the 1 to 10 miles they might need to traverse in order to reach a supermarket can pose an additional logistical problem when it comes to retrieving and returning food to the home.[4]

Many analysts have noted that African Americans are disproportionately likely to live in a food desert and racial prejudice may play a role in the formation of food deserts. It has been noted that discrimination at the agricultural level, and at the municipal level, contribute to the nutritional difficulties in poorer African American neighborhoods and this links the food deserts issue to broader issues involving social justice.[5]

The Factors That Contribute to Food Deserts

One of the biggest factors influencing the creation of food deserts is the loss of local, independent businesses. For much of American history, there were no supermarkets or "big box" stores. Individuals obtained food by visiting local markets or grocery stores and meats were often obtained from a local butcher. Local markets and shops typically purchased their goods from local farmers or butchers and thus the local markets and shops formed part of a local ecosystem that supplied residents with groceries while also supporting local agriculture and production. The shift to industrialization and to the global food market changed the landscape of American communities and this created the food deserts that are now the focus of public health advocates.

Supermarkets, like the "big box" retail stores and like massive online merchants like Amazon, keep costs low by purchasing in large quantities and by purchasing from overseas, especially from countries where labor and production costs are lower or where the strength of the local economy, in comparison to the United States means that U.S. purchasers enjoy an advantage. This means that larger chains can provide savings and this draws in consumers, who value the ability to shave costs from their food budgets. When this occurs, local stores and groceries cannot compete in price and if even a small percentage of a local grocer's customers opt for the supermarket option, local groceries can quickly lose profitability and often quickly go out of business. In many cases, local shops that remain have little choice but to shift to offering lower quality packaged foods, because purchasing high quality or local options provides too little profit to sustain their businesses. The spread of big retail grocery stores therefore puts smaller markets and stores out of business or sees them shift to offering the same low-quality options that might be found at larger stores. Nutritious options and local options increasingly become luxury commodities available only through specialty stores. Supermarkets also disrupt this market, as many have shifted to offering "organic" or higher quality variations on their products. Because these large chains can purchase in bulk, they are typically able to offer these higher quality goods at a more competitive price than a local health food store or organic grocer.

Walmart is an example of one of the large chains that officers both home goods and groceries. Numerous studies have found that the establishment of a Walmart is correlated by the loss of local businesses and, ultimately, a decline in local and sustainable employment opportunities.[6] The fact that shopping at the supermarkets and big box chains is damaging to local communities has matriculated into mainstream consciousness, but residents in many areas cannot afford to make alternate choices, either financially or in terms of expending the extra effort that might be needed to shop at independent or local stores as opposed to obtaining all of one's goods at a Walmart or similar store.

Interestingly, activists who are trying to combat the food desert issue often advocate for opening more large grocery chains in vulnerable neighborhoods. While this seems to solve the problem for residents in terms of food availability, and provides affordable food, the establishment of a large-scale grocery store can put further pressure on local shops, convenience stores, and grocers and can ultimately exacerbate the problem. Further, those who lack the financial resources to afford specialty grocery items might find that the establishment of a supermarket chain in their neighborhood provides access to food, but doesn't improve their capability to obtain higher quality or nutritious foods. Further, when a large chain is established in a community, and drives out remaining local options, the community becomes increasingly dependent on one or a few local retail options. If a Walmart moves into a community, followed by the closure of local competitors, the community is then extremely vulnerable to disruption if the Walmart in their area closes. If this happens, the community not only becomes a food desert, but residents may be worse off than they were before the large supermarket retailer was established in the area.

The goal of establishing grocery chains in food deserts has also proven extremely difficult. Though supermarket chains are designed to appeal to consumers at a variety of income levels, corporations operating the chains are often reluctant to try and establish stores in areas that are classified as food deserts. This is because these areas typically have lower levels of income, or lower population density, or other factors that limit the potential success of retailers trying to establish stores in that area. Under the Obama Administration, there was a major push to fill the food deserts by granting large chains economic advantages to move into underserved areas, but the large chains, in many cases, were still reluctant to try and establish new retail locations in many of those areas.[7]

In some cases, food deserts are the product of transportation issues. Because food deserts are related to the distance a person must travel to obtain food, individuals living in communities that are underserved by public transportation, or where infrastructure project have disrupted transportation options, may find themselves living in a food desert simply because there are no viable transportation options that would allow residents to reach the nearest grocery store or supermarket. Some advocates working to close food deserts have suggested that improving transportation options might be a better solution than trying to expand supermarket chains. This may be accomplished by expanding or changing bus routes or other transport options. Urban and suburban sprawl have contributed to food deserts because new housing projects may be located further and further from the nearest grocery store locations.[8] In some cities, problems finding parking or the cost of parking options also limit accessibility to food options.

Solutions and Perspectives

When considering solutions, it must be remembered that the goal in combating food deserts isn't just to provide access to food, but also to provide affordable access to high quality nutrition. A typical solution proposed to deal with a food desert is to encourage a supermarket chain to open a new branch or to expand operations into an underserved area. This solution, however, may not have the desired effect.

The corporatization of America's food culture is one of the reasons that food deserts exist. Supplanting local produce, vegetables, and meats with prepackaged and processed options reduced the quality and nutritional value of much of the food available across the country. Large-scale grocery chains may offer healthier or more nutritious items, but such items often cost more and are not as convenience to use as processed options. Individuals who have become accustomed to processed and unhealthy eating options may have little familiarity with how to choose and use healthier food items and thus there is a sociological and educational gulf involved in the food desert problem as well. Further, not all food deserts are created equal. There are some food deserts, in rural and suburban areas, that are the result of urban growth and sprawl. Residents in these areas may lack convenience access to food options, but may still possess the economic resources to afford better options. In such an environment, food delivery or local health food chains may provide an option, though posing an additional cost. For working class residents in other food deserts, higher priced local chains or food delivery options may not be workable solutions, because of the additional cost.

There are a number of organizations operating at the local level who have proposed independent solutions, such as investing in community gardens to allow residents to supplement their household food supplies with locally-grown fare. Local solutions, such as community farmer's markets, food delivery programs, or food co-ops can, in some cases, provide far better and healthier options for families than the relocation or establishment of large-scale supermarket chains. In addition, municipalities and states can subsidize food delivery programs or other means of providing better access to individuals facing additional problems accessing food options, such as the elderly or people living with disabilities. These solutions, while requiring community and municipal cooperation, can be better tailored for the specific challenges faced by residents of various food deserts and are likely more effective, over the longer term, than expanding supermarket chains.

Further, it can also be argued that more data is needed to properly understand all of the various factors involved. In a recent study published in the *Quarterly Journal of Economics*, researchers found that the establishment of new supermarkets did not result in residents of food deserts purchasing healthier food options, but simply resulted in providing easier access to the same low-quality options available before the establishment of the new supermarket. The authors of the study opined that nutrition education was one of the keys to bringing healthier nutrition to vulnerable neighborhoods and that this kind of education might be provided through schools, but also through alternative outreach programs that might be hosted at libraries or local farmer's markets, etc. Other methods, such as placing additional taxes on unhealthy foods, can also have an impact, both discouraging consumers from opting for these options and, potentially, discouraging food providers from investing in selling unhealthy products as well.[9]

There is no simple solution for the food desert issue, because there are so many contributing factors that play a role in how food deserts are initially created. In many ways, investing in local businesses and in local food options may provide the best, long-term solution to closing food deserts and to encouraging families to eat healthier. Whereas there are some issues within the broader issue of hunger in America where large scale policies might be needed, the food desert issues is one in which local solutions, tailored for specific areas, might be not only more effective, but more sustainable in terms of changing local culture to support and embrace the need for better more nutritious food options.

Works Used

Brones, Anna. "Food Apartheid: The Root of the Problem with America's Groceries." *The Guardian*. May 15, 2018. https://www.theguardian.com/society/2018/may/15/food-apartheid-food-deserts-racism-inequality-america-karen-washington-interview.

Costley, A. "Aging in a Food Desert: Differences in Food Access among Older and Younger Adults." *Innovation in Aging*, vol. 2, no. 1, 2018.

Devitt, James. "What Really Happens When a Grocery Store Opens in a 'Food Desert'?" *NYU*. Dec 10, 2019. https://www.nyu.edu/about/news-publications/news/2019/december/what-really-happens-when-a-grocery-store-opens-in-a--food-desert.html.

Frndak, Seth E. "Food-Deserts and Their Relationship with Academic Achievement in School Children." *ProQuest Dissertations Publishing*. Buffalo: University of New York, 2014.

Green, Dymond. "Why Food Deserts Are Still a Problem in America." *CNBC*. Aug 20, 2020. https://www.cnbc.com/2020/08/20/trader-joes-kroger-walmart-super-valu-and-americas-food-deserts.html.

"Grocery Chains Leave Food Deserts Barren, AP Analysis Finds." *Chicago Tribune*. Dec 7, 2015. https://www.chicagotribune.com/business/ct-grocery-chains-ig-nore-food-deserts-20151207-story.html.

Neumark, David, Junfu Zhang, and Stephen Ciccarella. "The Effects of Wal-Mart on Local Labor Markets." *Journal of Urban Economics*. Elsevier, 2008. http://www.economics.uci.edu/~dneumark/walmart.pdf.

Varney, Vincent. "The Solution to Food Deserts Isn't More Supermarkets—It's Better Transport." *Here 360*. Sep 30, 2019. https://360.here.com/food-deserts.

Walsan, Ramya, Nagesh B. Pai, and Biju Rajan. "Food Deserts and Its Impact on Mental Health." *Indian Journal of Social Psychiatry*, 2016.

Notes

1. Green, "Why Food Deserts Are Still a Problem in America."
2. Frndak, "Food-Deserts and Their Relationship with Academic Achievement in School Children."
3. Walsan, Pai, and Rajan, "Food Deserts and Its Impact on Mental Health."
4. Costley, "Aging in a Food Desert: Differences in Food Access among Older and Younger Adults."
5. Brones, "Food Apartheid: The Root of the Problem with America's Groceries."
6. Neumark, Zhang, and Ciccarella, "The Effects of Wal-Mart on Local Labor Markets."
7. "Grocery Chains Leave Food Deserts Barren, AP Analysis Finds," *Chicago Tribune*.
8. Varney, "The Solution to Food Deserts Isn't More Supermarkets—It's Better Transport."
9. Devitt, "What Really Happens When a Grocery Store Opens in a 'Food Desert'?"

Everything You Need to Know About Food Deserts

By Jessica Booth
Redbook, April 29, 2019

Staying healthy isn't just about working out and investing in self-care. A balanced diet is an incredibly important way to prevent diseases and health issues that could impact you in the long-term. According to the World Health Organization, a healthy diet includes plenty of fruits and vegetables, whole proteins, legumes, and beans. This can be easy enough to achieve if you're shopping correctly at the grocery store.

But what happens if you don't have access to some of these foods, or a store that sells them? In that case, you're probably going to eat whatever is available to you, whether it's healthy or not, something that can have a negative affect on your body. This kind of predicament is known as a food desert, and it's an issue everyone needs to be aware of.

What Exactly Is a Food Desert?

A food desert can be hard to define, but in general, the Centers for Disease Control and Prevention say that it's an area that lacks access to affordable foods that make up a healthy, balanced diet. This usually includes foods like fresh fruits and vegetables, low-fat milk, and whole grains, among others. Because people who live in food deserts don't have a reliable grocery store or farmers market to go to to buy these types of food, they often end up purchasing items at convenience stores or gas stations, where the options are not nearly as nutritious as they should be, or they're too expensive to afford.

Where Are Food Deserts Usually Found?

The United States Department of Agriculture says that a place is thought of as a food desert if the area meets certain low-income and low-access thresholds. If there's a poverty rate of 20% or greater, and at least 500 persons and/or 33% of the population lives more than a mile away from a supermarket or large grocery store, it's considered a food desert. The latest statistics from 2006 data show that an estimated 13.5 million people in the United States have low access to a proper grocery store, and 82% of them live in urban areas.

Who Is Most Affected?

In simple terms, the people most affected by food deserts are those who don't have access to large grocery stores where healthy options are available and affordable. But, of course, it's more complicated than just where someone lives. There are plenty of people who live in food deserts who also own cars—these people are able to get in their cars and drive to the grocery store, so they have more access. It's the people who don't have cars who are more affected, in that case. The USDA shows that about 2.3 million, or 2.2%, of households in the United States who live more than a mile from the grocery store also don't have access to a car.

Even public transportation doesn't necessarily make things easier all the time. As Food Empowerment Project points out, people in urban areas who are far from a grocery store may have very limited access to public transportation, or they don't have the money to take the required buses and/or trains.

Food deserts are also more likely to be found in communities with a high percentage of people of color. Studies have found that wealthy districts can have three times as many supermarkets as more low-income districts have. Other research has shown that white neighborhoods can have about four times as many supermarkets are predominantly black neighborhoods do, and on top of that, the supermarkets in black communities usually have less of a selection.

There Are Other Factors That Make a Place a Food Desert

While socio-economic status is definitely a big part of what makes a place a food desert to begin with, there are other factors that go into it as well. The USDA says that many places lack large grocery stores because companies just don't want to build there. There are a lot of reasons they're avoiding the area: the costs that come with building

> **A food desert is an area that lacks access to affordable foods that make up a healthy, balanced diet.**

there (for example, if the rent or price of land is higher), the zoning rules that come with building there, their location in terms of convenient delivery routes, and the crime and security concerns associated with the area. They also take into account the buying habits and demographic and economic characteristics of consumers in the area.

This is all especially true for large supermarkets, which need a lot of land and parking, as well as the ability to accommodate large trucks. This is one of the reasons food deserts can be found in urban areas or very small towns.

Serious Negative Health Consequences Come with Food Deserts

Research shows that people who live in food deserts often can't find culturally appropriate food, can't find food that fits into their dietary restrictions (if they are lactose intolerant, for example), and can't afford the little healthy food that they do have access to. Because of this, they are essentially forced into eating unhealthy options, like frozen foods, highly processed foods, and fast food. At the end of the day, 55% of people in food deserts are less likely to have a good-quality diet over people who live elsewhere.

Because food deserts mainly affect quality of food over actual access to food, the biggest health concern associated with food deserts has often been obesity, something that comes with eating unhealthy options on a regular basis. Obesity can cause a variety of health issues, such as high blood pressure, diabetes, heart disease, stroke, cancer, and mental disorders.

Food deserts have a particularly negative affect on children as well, who need to have a healthy diet in the first few years of their life in order to develop properly. When a kid has poor nutrition, they can be at risk for obesity and all that comes with it, iron deficiencies, dental cavities, and long-term health effects that go into adulthood, like a higher risk of cancer and high blood pressure.

It's also important to consider the people in food deserts who have dietary restrictions that can't be met because of their limited access to supermarkets. These people are often forced into eating food they're allergic to, which can lead to them being seriously sick and needing emergency treatment.

How Can We Get Rid of Food Deserts or Prevent Them from Happening in the First Place?

Tackling the issue of food deserts is a tough one, but some initiatives are already in place. The Healthy Food Financing Initiative was started in 2010 in an attempt to bring grocery stores and healthier options to food deserts. Michelle Obama's Let's Move Act, which brought salad bars to schools across the country, was also aiding in preventing and getting rid of food deserts.

The CDC also recommends that the people in these communities participate in the efforts by establishing a community garden and/or organizing local farmers markets. Local governments should be improving transportation to get people easier access to the closest supermarkets, and changing the tough zoning codes and taxes that keep businesses away from the area.

It would also help if healthier food was made more affordable. Research has shown that the price of fruits and vegetables increased almost 75% between 1989 and 2005, and at the same time, the price of fatty foods decreased by more than 26%. If healthy food is going to continue to be more inexpensive, it's still not going to be accessible to low-income shoppers, whether they have access to the grocery store or not.

Educating People on the Importance of Eating Healthy Food Is Just as Important

Unfortunately, eradicating the problems associated with food deserts isn't as easy as giving the people who live in them access to supermarkets. A 2018 Chicago Booth study found that giving people in low-income households the same products and prices as people in high-income households reduced nutritional inequality by only 9%.

Some studies have even shown that food deserts do not correlate with obesity. A 2017 study found that improved food access doesn't show "strong evidence toward enhancing health-related outcomes over short durations."

So, the answer to food deserts isn't just about increasing access to supermarkets and healthier food prices. It's also about educating people on how to eat better. Experts believe that the focus needs to be more on helping people make better personal choices when it comes to food, rather than just giving them access to healthier food.

This is a reminder of how important proper food education is. Access to healthier foods is a good step for food deserts, but making sure people know what they should be buying and eating is even more essential.

Print Citations

CMS: Booth, Jessica. "Everything You Need to Know About Food Deserts." In *The Reference Shelf: Food Insecurity & Hunger in the United States,* edited by Micah L. Issitt, 65-68. Amenia, NY: Grey House Publishing, 2021.

MLA: Booth, Jessica. "Everything You Need to Know About Food Deserts." *The Reference Shelf: Food Insecurity & Hunger in the United States,* edited by Micah L. Issitt, Grey House Publishing, 2021, pp. 65-68.

APA: Booth, J. (2021). Everything you need to know about food deserts. In Micah L. Issitt (Ed.), *The reference shelf: Food insecurity & hunger in the United States* (pp. 65-68). Amenia, NY: Grey House Publishing.

Eliminating Food Deserts Won't Help Poorer Americans Eat Healthier

By Hunt Allcott, Jean-Pierre Dubé, and Molly Schnell
The Conversation, December 1, 2019

In the U.S., rich people tend to eat a lot healthier than poor people.

Because poor diets cause obesity, Type II diabetes and other diseases, this nutritional inequality contributes to unequal health outcomes. The richest Americans can expect to live 10-15 years longer than the poorest.

Many think that a key cause of nutritional inequality is food deserts—or neighborhoods without supermarkets, mostly in low-income areas. The narrative is that folks who live in food deserts are forced to shop at local convenience stores, where it's hard to find healthy groceries. If we could just get a supermarket to open in those neighborhoods, the thinking goes, then people would be able to eat healthy.

The data tell a strikingly different story.

Negligible Change

We recently studied the impact of opening supermarkets in food deserts in research conducted with fellow economists Rebecca Diamond, Jessie Handbury and Ilya Rahkovsky.

From 2004 to 2016, over 1,000 supermarkets opened in neighborhoods around the country that previously had been food deserts. We analyzed the grocery purchases of a sample of 10,000 households living in those neighborhoods.

Did they start to buy healthier food after the supermarket opened nearby?

Although many people began shopping at the new local supermarket after it opened, they generally didn't buy healthier food. We can statistically conclude that the effect on healthy eating from opening new supermarkets was negligible at best. We calculated that local access to supermarkets explains no more than about 1.5% of the difference in healthy eating between low- and high-income households.

How could this be?

Why Food Deserts Aren't the Problem

The food desert narrative suggests the lack of supply of healthy foods is what causes reduced demand for them.

But in the modern economy, stores have become amazingly good at selling us exactly the kinds of things we want to buy. Our research suggests the opposite narrative: Lower demand for healthy food is what causes the lack of supply.

> **Although many people began shopping at the new local supermarket after it opened, they generally didn't buy healthier food.**

Furthermore, local neighborhood conditions don't matter much, since we regularly venture outside our neighborhoods. We calculate that the average American travels 5.2 miles to shop. Low-income households aren't that different: They travel 4.8 miles.

Given that we're willing to travel that far, we tend to shop in supermarkets even if there isn't one down the street. We found that even people who live in ZIP codes without a supermarket still buy 85% of their groceries from supermarkets.

Tax Sugar, Subsidize Produce

In other words, people don't suddenly go from shopping at an unhealthy convenience store to shopping at the new, healthy supermarket. In reality, people go from shopping at a faraway supermarket to shopping at a new supermarket that offers the same types of groceries.

To be clear, new grocery stores do provide many benefits. In many neighborhoods, new retail can bring jobs, a place to see neighbors and a sense of revitalization. People who live nearby get more options and don't have to travel as far to shop.

But the data show that healthier eating is not one of those benefits.

Instead, we would recommend tweaking prices as a better approach to encouraging healthier habits. Taxes on sugary drinks can discourage their consumption, while food-stamp programs could be modified to make fruits and vegetables cheaper.

And, given that we develop long-term eating habits as children, parents and schools can encourage kids to eat healthier.

Health inequality is one of our society's most important problems. We hope that this research can direct efforts toward ideas that can materially improve health—and away from ideas that do not.

Print Citations

CMS: Allcott, Hunt, Jean-Pierre Dubé, and Molly Schnell. "Eliminating Food Deserts Won't Help Poorer Americans Eat Healthier." In *The Reference Shelf: Food Insecurity & Hunger in the United States,* edited by Micah L. Issitt, 69-71. Amenia, NY: Grey House Publishing, 2021.

MLA: Allcott, Hunt, Jean-Pierre Dubé, and Molly Schnell. "Eliminating Food Deserts Won't Help Poorer Americans Eat Healthier." *The Reference Shelf: Food Insecurity & Hunger in the United States,* edited by Micah L. Issitt, Grey House Publishing, 2021, pp. 69-71.

APA: Allcott, H., Dubé, J.-P., & Schnell, M. (2021). Eliminating food deserts won't help poorer Americans eat healthier. In Micah L. Issitt (Ed.), *The reference shelf: Food insecurity & hunger in the United States* (pp. 69-71). Amenia, NY: Grey House Publishing.

The Fight to Eliminate Food Deserts in St. Louis

By Rebecca Koenig
Sauce Magazine, October 31, 2017

Antwan Pope has a vision. Whzen the social services specialist surveys his Wells Goodfellow neighborhood, he sees fertile ground for a food revolution. The Wellston Station, a century-old, open-air pavilion where streetcars once stopped at the city limits, has what Pope calls a ready-made "farmers market atmosphere," complete with a Chuck Berry mural. Nearby vacant lots seem perfectly suited for community gardens where residents could grow their own produce.

And of course, Pope sees plenty of room for a grocery store—a full-service one where his 88-year-old grandmother could shop for fruits and vegetables instead of traveling two miles to Schnucks City Plaza.

"She shouldn't have to do that," he said.

Pope's plan for reviving the intersection of Hodiamont Avenue and Dr. Martin Luther King Drive is evidence of the activism at work throughout St. Louis, intended to create more equitable access to affordable, healthy food.

The area is plagued by food deserts—neighborhoods without a Dierbergs, Shop 'n Save or Aldi in sight. Most of their inhabitants are people of color. In the city, nine census tracts have significant numbers of low-income residents who live at least a mile from a grocery store, according to 2015 data from the U.S. Department of Agriculture Economic Research Service. There are 22 such tracts in St. Louis County. Change that distance to a half-mile, and dozens more communities qualify as deserts.

That distance might not sound like such a big deal, but it matters especially to people who don't have cars. In Wells Goodfellow, about one-fifth of households lack personal vehicles, which means residents are dependent on public transportation— or their own two feet—to get to supermarkets elsewhere. Walking a mile is easy if you're in good health, but think about how hard it can be to unload groceries when you're just carrying bags from the car to your kitchen counter. Now imagine making the trip on foot as an 88-year-old, or while carrying your child, or dependent on a wheelchair. Even those cute, foldable personal shopping carts wouldn't be much help, considering that to trek the 1.7 miles from Wellston Station to the nearest grocery store–a Save-A-Lot–you have to hike through overgrown lots or trod carefully on the road's edge because the sidewalk disappears.

Incapable of making such a trip as often as they need to and tired of subsisting on meager gas station selections, desert dwellers are increasingly looking inward to improve their food access. They're teaming up with advocates in academia and development to devise innovative economic solutions. They're figuring out new ways to tap the resources their neighborhoods already have, most notably the corner stores that serve as lifelines on blocks with no other options. Why, they ask, should they have to go elsewhere to find milk and broccoli and whole-grain bread? Why can't healthy food come to them?

"With neighborhoods in St. Louis, there's a real opportunity to change food culture," said Bob Ray, part owner of the Washington Avenue Post market.

Swapping Out Sugar

If Walnut Park East is home, chances are you have trouble getting groceries. Like a quarter of your neighbors, you may not have a car, which means you take the bus to the nearest Save-A-Lot, which is miles away.

Much closer is the Regal Meat Market. For years, your family may have stopped by for chicken wings, gyros or hamburgers. The Hamed family, owners since 1998, takes pride in having you as a loyal customer. They may even give you a free Thanksgiving turkey.

If Regal stocked the same kinds of groceries as Save-A-Lot, it could significantly change the contents of your fridge.

So believes Kara Lubischer, specialist in healthy food access at the University of Missouri Extension. St. Louis is sprinkled with more than 250 corner, convenience and liquor stores, local institutions that serve as food sources for places like Walnut Park East. A few years ago, Lubischer recognized the potential these shops have to stand in for absent supermarkets.

"Instead of going after the shiny and new, I saw this as an opportunity to go after what we already have," she said.

In 2011, Lubischer led a team to develop the St. Louis Healthy Corner Store Project. Designed to increase both the demand for and the supply of nutritious food in small neighborhood markets, it relied on the expertise of store owners, community organizers, city officials and customers.

The primary goal was modest: increase the amount of healthy food on corner store shelves by 5 percent. That meant reduced-fat milk instead of whole milk, water instead of soda and whole-grain products instead of processed sugar snacks.

Lubischer knew imposing programs on communities from the outside rarely works well. So she and her team went to churches, neighborhood associations and schools, asking locals

Project leaders knew it was essential to educate customers in order to increase demand for the items store owners were stocking.

to nominate stores they'd like to participate. The community council of Walbridge Elementary nominated Regal Meat Market.

Although such nominations were flattering, alone they weren't always enough to incentivize store owners. After all, "businesses are in business to make money," Ray said.

So project leaders provided marketing support like signs, produce bins and customer loyalty cards. They talked up the fact that corner stores can make profit margins on dairy, bread, meat and produce ranging from 25 to 50 percent. And they explained that some participating stores were eligible for grants to improve their facades with new awnings and repaired windows.

Ultimately, nine store owners signed on.

"It was sort of a brave thing for them to do," Lubischer said. "They were running their businesses just fine before the university and the health department showed up."

Ray came on board to talk shop with other store owners, sharing his institutional knowledge about which grocery distributors offer fair prices to independent markets and how to make a profit off healthy goods. Owners were often wary of stocking perishable food that might spoil before it sold. Ray told his mentees that bananas are a safe bet.

"People are bananas about bananas," he said. "Our store goes through two cases, with 13 bunches per case, every week. We sell a single banana for 59 cents."

That lesson resonated with Majd Hamed at Regal Meat Market. Previously, bananas hadn't sold well there, so Ray suggested moving them closer to the registers so they'd become impulse purchases.

"We stuck to it, and I can't keep up with bananas no more," Hamed said. "We put them on the counter in the front, and oh my God, the bananas don't even get to turn yellow."

Experimentation has since taught Hamed that red grapes are big sellers, while "white grapes sit and rot and I'll lose my money." Lemons go quickly, but cabbage is hit or miss; some weeks it sells, other weeks it gets old and has to be tossed.

Project leaders knew it was essential to educate customers in order to increase demand for the items store owners were stocking.

"You can't just stick healthy food in the neighborhood and have people start buying it without having any idea it's there or having any idea what to do with it," said Mary Wissmann, a nutritionist who works with the university extension program.

Stores hosted healthy product taste tests and cooking demonstrations using recipes that called only for ingredients available on the shelves. There were nutrition classes in senior centers, churches and community centers near the participating corner stores. Tailored to address community concerns like diabetes and early childhood nutrition, the courses taught important skills including reading labels, shopping on a budget and preparing meals. Healthy Corner Store Project representatives attended the classes to inform people their local markets had started stocking relevant items.

To make the program more sustainable, project leaders wanted to encourage customers to give owners direct feedback about products they'd like to buy. They set up poster boards in each store labeled with the question, "What healthy foods would you like to see here?"

Regal Meat Market had been trying unsuccessfully to sell whole watermelons. When its poster board went up, someone wrote, "cut watermelon." Other customers circled the recommendation, then starred it.

So the Hameds cut up the melons, put the pieces into plastic cups and attached forks. The handy snacks started selling immediately–a sweet, yet wholesome, alternative to candy.

Bringing Back the Bounty

By 2015, after four years in operation, results from the St. Louis Healthy Corner Store Project were promising. Some stores ended up with 25 percent more healthy inventory, far surpassing the 5 percent goal.

Of course, some parts of St. Louis lack even corner stores.

When Pope decided in 2014 to rehabilitate the Wellston Station corner through youth meal and activity programs, "there was no produce, no fresh fruit, no kind of vegetation in the area, period," he said. Student volunteers from Washington University and the University of Missouri–St. Louis who came to help with clean-up days all noticed there were no stores–other than a laundromat, a pawn shop and a Family Dollar.

Leaders at Operation Food Search, a food distribution nonprofit, confirmed to Pope that the area is indeed a food desert. That wasn't always the case. The neighborhood once had a thriving business district. Observers in 1941 noted an abundance of "open stalls for vegetables and flowers, crates of chickens and geese, and the tantalizing odors of herring and dill." One of Pope's elderly neighbors enjoys recalling the days when jobs–and produce stands–were plentiful near Wells Goodfellow.

Pope is determined to coax that kind of bounty back into his community. There are signs of progress, like the several community gardens planted among the neighborhood's houses.

Ray believes these gardens, and more substantial established urban farms, have the potential to change his neighborhood's relationship with food. That is, if they're invested in. "Instead of a food desert, we could be raising food in these communities because of all this vacant land," he said. "We could be creating jobs and opportunity."

Other St. Louisans have taken up the charge. In The Grove, City Greens Market offers produce, meat and other products from Missouri and Illinois to members who pay on a sliding income scale. The nonprofit co-op evolved out of a CSA program in the basement of St. Cronan Church, created by women tired of making multiple bus transfers to get to supermarkets.

This fall, the Wellston and North Hanley MetroLink transit centers will boast brand-new markets selling produce, pantry staples and refrigerated items. The

University of Missouri Extension will provide nutrition education on-site at least once a month at each location.

And in January, Good Life Growing, a Vandeventer farm that uses hydroponic, aquaponic and aeroponic systems, plans to open Old North Provisions, a mixed-use restaurant and grocery store.

Pope is excited that Metro Market, a bus-turned-mobile-produce-stand that has occasionally come to Wells Goodfellow, is hoping to add the area to its regular rotation next year. The market specializes in low-cost, local produce and is participating in the Double Up Food Bucks program, which allows customers spending food assistance benefits to double their money on fruits and veggies.

"When they pulled that bus on that corner, oh my God," Pope said. "They literally sold all the stuff they had on this bus out."

Local Lessons, National Legacy

Financial support for the St. Louis Healthy Corner Store Project, which came from the Missouri Foundation for Health, the Missouri Department of Health and Senior Services and a Community Development Block Grant administered by St. Louis Development Corporation, ran out in 2015. The project ended.

Its leaders used the lessons they'd learned to create a similar, Missouri-wide program called Stock Healthy, Shop Healthy. Lubischer oversees the program, which operates in 14 counties and counting, from Kansas City.

Seven other states have emulated the new program. St. Louis, Lubischer said, deserves full credit for its success.

"We learned great things from our store owners. They taught us so much," she added. It's possible that the corner store program will return to St. Louis, if the right local partner champions it. Whether the model can sustain itself and how much it could transform food deserts, though, depends on who you ask. Some corner stores have trouble processing food assistance benefits, for instance, which reduces their usefulness to many customers.

Corner stores will never become Whole Foods, Lubischer cautions. Rather, she hopes businesses like Regal Meat Market will stock enough tomatoes and whole-grain bread to sustain families without ready access to a car until their next major supermarket trip.

Such markets need advocates in local and state government, Ray believes, especially when so much support already goes to major enterprises like the Schnucks Culinara.

"It would be better to support small businesses, help them become nice little markets, than it would to support multimillion-dollar companies that don't need the help," he said. "We should be setting up co-ops to give some of these smaller businesses buying power to buy bulk purchases in order to be competitive. It's almost impossible to compete. It just is."

Years after the St. Louis Healthy Corner Store Project's official end, Regal Meat Market still moves a lot of potatoes, lettuce, apples, oranges, tomatoes and green peppers. Hamed spoke favorably of the project's goals, but lamented the difficulty the store has had marketing healthy goods to younger customers, who he said still seem to prefer "junk food."

"If it wasn't for the old people who come here and cook, a lot of my stuff would go to waste," he said.

Still, one of the strong sellers at Regal Meat Market is a holdover from the Healthy Corner Store Project. A few years ago, on the advice of project leaders, the Hameds used a donated chalkboard sidewalk sign to advertise a new prepared food product: fresh chicken salad.

"That worked," Hamed said, "bringing us different clientele: healthy food eaters."

Why are food deserts a problem?

There are 9 St. Louis city and 22 St. Louis County census tracts that qualify as food deserts, with residents–primarily low-income people of color–living at least 1 mile from a grocery store. In some of these neighborhoods, 20 percent of households don't have a car and there are 0 sidewalks. Try walking a mile on the side of a busy road lugging 50 pounds of groceries in fragile plastic bags. Now imagine you're elderly, disabled or caring fulltime for your children.

Businesses and organizations working to eradicate St. Louis food deserts

City Greens Market 4260 Manchester Ave., St. Louis, 314.884.8460, stlcitygreens.org

Good Life Growing 4057 Evans Ave., St. Louis, goodlifegrowing.com

Old North Provisions 2720 N. 14th St., St. Louis (opening 2018)

Operation Food Search operationfoodsearch.org

Regal Meat Market 5791 Thekla Ave., St. Louis, 314.382.8509

St. Louis Metro Market stlmetromarket.com

Stock Healthy, Shop Healthy extension.missouri.edu/stockhealthy

Washington Avenue Post 1315 Washington Ave., St. Louis, 314.588.0545, Facebook: Washington Ave Post

Print Citations

CMS: Koenig, Rebecca. "The Fight to Eliminate Food Deserts in St. Louis." In *The Reference Shelf: Food Insecurity & Hunger in the United States,* edited by Micah L. Issitt, 72-77. Amenia, NY: Grey House Publishing, 2021.

MLA: Koenig, Rebecca. "The Fight to Eliminate Food Deserts in St. Louis." *The Reference Shelf: Food Insecurity & Hunger in the United States,* edited by Micah L. Issitt, Grey House Publishing, 2021, pp. 72-77.

APA: Koenig, R. (2021). The fight to eliminate food deserts in St. Louis. In Micah L. Issitt (Ed.), *The reference shelf: Food insecurity & hunger in the United States* (pp. 72-77). Amenia, NY: Grey House Publishing.

It's Not the Food Deserts: It's the Inequality

By Richard Florida
CityLab, January 18, 2018

Too many Americans are overweight and eat unhealthy food, a problem that falls disproportionately on poor and low-income people. For many urbanists, the main culprit has long been "food deserts"—disadvantaged neighborhoods that are underserved by quality grocery stores, and where people's nutritional options are limited to cheaper, high-calorie, and less nutritious food.

But a new study by economists at New York University, Stanford University, and the University of Chicago adds more evidence to the argument that food deserts alone are not to blame for the eating habits of people in low-income neighborhoods. The biggest difference in what we eat comes not from where we live per se, but from deeper, more fundamental differences in income and, especially, in education and nutritional knowledge, which shape our eating habits and in turn impact our health.

To gauge the quality of food and nutrition by income groups and across different geographies, the study uses data from the Nielsen Homescan panel on purchases of groceries and packaged food and drink items between 2004 and 2015, which it then evaluates in terms of the U.S. Department of Agriculture's Healthy Eating Index. It studies the gap between high- and low-income households: namely, those with annual incomes of $70,000 or more, and low-income households with incomes of less than $25,000 per year.

The study reinforces the notion that food deserts are disproportionately found in disadvantaged neighborhoods. It finds that more than half (55 percent) of all ZIP codes with a median income below $25,000 fit the definition of food deserts—that's more than double the share of food-desert ZIP codes across the country as a whole (24 percent).

Furthermore, the study documents the disturbing extent of nutritional inequality in America. Across the board, high-income households benefit from better, more nutritious food. They buy and consume more of the four very healthy food groups: fiber, protein, fruit, and vegetables. They also consume less of two of the four unhealthy food groups, saturated fat and sugar (their consumption of sodium and cholesterol is basically the same as that of lower-income households).

Indeed, the groceries of higher-income households are considerably healthier—in statistical terms, almost 0.3 standard deviations healthier—than those of low-income households, a gap which expanded substantially between 2004 and 2015. Overall, high-income households purchase one additional gram of fiber per 1,000 calories than low-income ones, which is associated with a 9.4 percent decrease in Type 2 diabetes. They also buy 3.5 fewer grams of sugar, which correlates with a 10 percent decrease in death rates from heart disease.

That said, there are some striking similarities in food consumption between high- and low-income households. They both mainly shop at grocery stores, no matter where they live. High-income households spend 91 percent of their grocery dollars at supermarkets. Low-income households spend just slightly less, at 87 percent.

Also, both high- and low-income households, including those living in food deserts, travel relatively similar distances to reach grocery stores. . . . The average American travels roughly 5.5 miles to buy their groceries. Low-income households travel slightly less distance, an average of 4.8 miles. Americans who live in food deserts across the board travel farther, an average of 7 miles or so. But that includes those who live in rural areas. Those in urban food deserts travel a bit less than the overall average, while low-income households that live in urban food deserts and do not own a car—the group that the food-desert argument is mainly about—travel just 2 miles on average.

So what is the role of neighborhood location in American diets, and why do food deserts matter far less than the conventional wisdom says they do?

To get at this, the study cleverly tracks two things. First, it looks at what happens when new supermarkets open in less-advantaged neighborhoods, including food deserts. It turns out that the entry of new supermarkets has little impact on the eating habits of low-income households. Even when people in these low-income neighborhoods do buy groceries from the new supermarkets, they tend to buy products of the same low nutritional value.

Basically, new, closer-by supermarkets simply divert sales from older, farther-away supermarkets. As the authors of the study succinctly put it, "supermarket entry does not significantly change choice sets, and thus doesn't affect healthy eating." Overall, improving neighborhood access to better grocery stores is responsible for just 5 percent of the difference in the nutritional choices of both high- and low-income people.

More than half of all zip codes with a median income below $25,000 fit the definition of food deserts.

Second, the study looks at what happens when low-income people move from neighborhoods served by lower-quality stores to ones with healthier offerings. Again, it finds little effect. Moving to a neighborhood where people have healthier eating habits has virtually no impact in the short term and a very small impact in the medium term, leading to just about a 3 percent improvement in the Healthy Eating Index scores of their grocery purchases.

Ultimately, the study finds little evidence to support the notion that food deserts are solely to blame for unhealthy eating. It concludes that the "evidence does not support the notion that eliminating food deserts would have material effects on nutritional inequality."

Instead of within cities, the biggest geographic differences in the way Americans eat occur across regions. . . . While there is some variation within cities and metro areas, by far the biggest and most obvious differences are across broad regions of the country. There is a large "unhealthy eating belt" across the Midwest and South, surrounded by healthier eating belts along the East Coast, West Coast, and Pacific Northwest.

Ultimately, the fundamental difference in America's food and nutrition has more to do with class than location. More than 90 percent of the difference in Americans' nutritional inequality is the product of socioeconomic class, according to the study. And it's not just that higher-income Americans have more money to spend on food. In fact, the cost of healthy food is not as prohibitively high as people tend to think. While healthy food costs a little bit more than unhealthy food, most of that is driven by the cost of fresh produce. There is only a marginal price difference between other healthy versus unhealthy eating options. Furthermore, the price gap between healthy and unhealthy food is actually a little bit lower than average in many low-income neighborhoods, according to the study.

When it comes to food and nutrition, it's not just that higher income Americans have more money. They benefit even more from higher levels of education and better information about the benefits of healthier eating. Indeed, education accounts for roughly 20 percent of the association between income and healthy eating, according to the study, with an additional 7 percent coming from differences in information about nutrition.

The authors of the study suggest that equipping less advantaged Americans with more knowledge and better information about healthy eating may be the better and more efficient path for policy, but I am less sanguine. Information on healthy eating is widely available. Calorie counts and ingredients are listed on many, if not most, food items.

There are deeper reasons, again tied to class, that enable affluent and educated households to put this nutritional information to use. For one, they simply have more time and resources to devote to their health and well-being. Conversely, lower-income people may simply discount the health advantages of higher-quality food or see some of those foods, like kale or avocado toast (to pick the most obvious examples), as smacking of urban elitism. This may explain why Trump's much-talked-about preferences for fast food and Diet Coke seem to resonate so well with his populist base.

Whatever the case, America's great nutritional divide reflects the fundamental class divisions of our society, mirroring very same class divide we see in fitness, obesity, and overall health and well-being. It's not food deserts per se, but this deeper fault line which is to blame for nutritional inequality, as it is for many of the other glaring inequities of American society today.

Print Citations

CMS: Florida, Richard. "It's Not the Food Deserts: It's the Inequality." In *The Reference Shelf: Food Insecurity & Hunger in the United States,* edited by Micah L. Issitt, 78-81. Amenia, NY: Grey House Publishing, 2021.

MLA: Florida, Richard. "It's Not the Food Deserts: It's the Inequality." *The Reference Shelf: Food Insecurity & Hunger in the United States,* edited by Micah L. Issitt, Grey House Publishing, 2021, pp. 78-81.

APA: Florida, R. (2021). It's not the food deserts: It's the inequality. In Micah L. Issitt (Ed.), *The reference shelf: Food insecurity & hunger in the United States* (pp. 78-81). Amenia, NY: Grey House Publishing.

The COVID-19 Crisis Has Already Left Too Many Children Hungry in America

By Lauren Bauer
Brookings, May 6, 2020

Since the onset of the COVID-19 pandemic, food insecurity has increased in the United States. This is particularly true for households with young children.

document new evidence from two nationally representative surveys that were initiated to provide up-to-date estimates of the consequences of the COVID-19 pandemic, including the incidence of food insecurity. Food insecurity occurs when a household has difficulty providing enough food due to a lack of resources.

The COVID Impact Survey and The Hamilton Project/Future of the Middle Class Initiative Survey of Mothers with Young Children asked validated questions taken from the U.S. Department of Agriculture's (USDA) food security question-naire in late April 2020. [i] Households and children are considered food insecure if the respondent indicates the following statements were often or sometimes true:

- The food we bought just didn't last and we didn't have enough money to get more.

- The children in my household were not eating enough because we just couldn't afford enough food.

To compare April 2020 estimates of food insecurity with statistics from earlier time points, I use the same questions listed above to replicate these results with the Current Population Survey Food Security Supplement (FSS), the source of USDA's official food insecurity statistics [ii]. . .

High levels of food insecurity [were] observed in the COVID Impact Survey and in the Survey of Mothers with Young Children. By the end of April, more than one in five households in the United States, and two in five households with mothers with children 12 and under, were food insecure. In almost one in five households of mothers with children age 12 and under, the children were experiencing food insecurity.

Rates of food insecurity observed in April 2020 are also meaningfully higher than at any point for which there is comparable data. . . . Looking over time, particularly to the relatively small increase in child food insecurity during the Great Recession, it is clear that young children are experiencing food insecurity to an extent unprec-edented in modern times.

Food Insecurity Has Deteriorated More among Households with Children

In the Survey of Mothers with Young Children, 17.4 percent of mothers with children ages 12 and under reported that since the pandemic started, "the children in my household were not eating enough because we just couldn't afford enough food." Of those mothers, 3.4 percent reported that it was *often* the case that their children were not eating enough due to a lack of resources since the coronavirus pandemic began.

By comparison, in the 2018 FSS, 3.1 percent of mothers with a child age 12 and under reported that their children were not eating enough because they could not afford enough food ever in the past twelve months. The incidence of hardship among children as measured by responses to this question has increased 460 percent.

But responses to this question alone do not fully capture child food insecurity. To estimate food insecurity, the USDA aggregates a battery of questions on access to food from the Current Population Survey. In total for 2018, 7.4 percent of mothers with children under the age of 12 had food insecure children in their household, more than double the share who said that the children in their household were not eating enough because they couldn't afford enough food (3.1 percent). If the ratio between this single question and the overall measure of child food insecurity were to continue to hold today, 17.4 percent children not eating enough would translate into more than a third of children experiencing food insecurity.

The Survey of Mothers with Young Children found that 40.9 percent of mothers with children ages 12 and under reported household food insecurity since the onset of the COVID-19 pandemic. This is higher than the rate reported by all respondents with children under twelve in the COVID Impact Survey (34.4 percent) but the same as women 18–59 living with a child 12 and under (39.2 percent.) In 2018, 15.1 percent of mothers with children ages 12 and under affirmatively answered this question in the FSS, slightly more than the 14.5 percent that were

> **Food insecurity occurs when a household has difficulty providing enough food due to a lack of resources.**

food insecure by the complete survey. The share of mothers with children 12 and under reporting that the food that they bought did not last has increased 170 percent.

Food insecurity in households with children under 18 has increased by about 130 percent from 2018 to today. Using the COVID Impact Survey, I find that 34.5 percent of households with a child 18 and under were food insecure as of late April 2020. On this single question ("the food we bought didn't last...") in the 2018 FSS, 14.7 percent of households with children 18 and under affirmatively answered this question; this value is slightly higher than the overall rate of food insecurity among households with children 18 and under for that year.

High levels of food insecurity are not just a problem of households with children. Prior to the crisis, in 2018, 11.1 percent of households were food insecure and 12.2

percent of households answered the single question in the battery affirmatively. The Urban Institute's Health Reform Monitoring Survey, in the field from March 25 to April 10, used the six-question short form food insecurity module and found that 21.9 percent of households with nonelderly adults were food insecure. By late April 2020, 22.7 percent of households reported in the COVID Impact Survey not having sufficient resources to buy more food when the food that they purchased didn't last. Overall rates of household food insecurity have effectively doubled.

Families Need More Resources to Handle These Material Hardships

Policymakers must act to protect the health and well-being of the American people, especially children.

Luckily, food insecurity is an unusual policy challenge in that it recommends a clear solution. To reduce the number of people, including children, who have insufficient food due to a lack of resources, policymakers can supply the resources.

To increase food security, economic security, and economic stimulus, Congress should increase the generosity of food security programs immediately and ensure that benefits levels stay elevated consistent with economic data. Governors should work with USDA to implement these programs. Specifically:

Increase maximum Supplemental Nutrition Assistance Program (SNAP, formerly the Food Stamp program) benefits by at least 15 percent and double the minimum benefit;

- Provide SNAP emergency allotments, authorized under Families First, to those households that are eligible to receive the maximum level of benefits (more than 5 million children reside in these households and they have received no additional SNAP benefits during this crisis);

- Extend Pandemic-EBT through this summer and through at least the end of the 2020-2021 school year to ensure there are sufficient resources to purchase food in the event of ongoing schooling disruptions (Pandemic-EBT is a new program which provides the value of school meals as a grocery voucher to eligible families when schools are closed, a little more than $100 per child per month);

- Support families with children ages 5 and under through an additional SNAP multiplier or by broadening eligibility for Pandemic-EBT; and,

- Suspend SNAP work requirements for students and sustain the ABAWD SNAP work requirement suspension.

At the very beginning of the COVID-19 crisis, Diane Schanzenbach and I called for "at least" a 15 percent benefit increase to SNAP. Evidence presented in this piece reiterates that a 15 percent increase to SNAP should be the floor.

New nationally representative surveys fielded since the pandemic began show that rates of food insecurity overall, among households with children, and among children themselves are higher than they have ever been on record. Food insecurity represents an urgent matter for policymakers in the capitol and in state houses across the country. Food security programs, centrally SNAP and Pandemic-EBT, must be strengthened and expanded immediately.

[i] The COVID Impact Survey is a nationally representative survey conducted by NORC at the University of Chicago on behalf of the Data Foundation; it uses the AmeriSpeak panel and was in the field from April 20 to April 26, 2020. The Hamilton Project and the Future of the Middle Class Initiative, both affiliates of the Brookings Institution, conducted a nationally representative survey of mothers with children ages 12 and under using SurveyMonkey from April 27 to April 28, 2020. Technical documentation for the COVID Impact Survey can be found here. The Survey of Mothers with Young Children was developed by Lauren Bauer and Richard Reeves; Katherine Guyot and Emily Moss contributed substantially to the development of the survey and we acknowledge the contributions of The Hamilton Project, Future of Middle Class Initiative, and Economic Studies staff at the Brookings Institution. Both surveys used an iterative raking procedure to adjust the surveyed data to match demographic weighting variables obtained from the 2020 Current Population Survey. The COVID Impact Survey was weighted to reflect the U.S. population 18 and over while the Survey of Mothers with Young Children was weighted to reflect the population of mothers with at least one of their own children age 12 and under in their household. Additional technical documentation regarding the Survey of Mothers with Young Children is available from the author.

[ii] While this is a cleaner approach than comparisons to the complete food insecurity battery, the food insecurity time period about which the three surveys ask are each different. I have presented the most conservative estimates throughout this piece, comparing affirmative responses on single questions from the food insecurity battery for the last twelve months (FSS), the last 30 days (COVID Impact Study), and since the coronavirus pandemic began (Survey of Mothers with Young Children). Additional analyses are available from the author.

Print Citations

CMS: Bauer, Lauren. "The COVID-19 Crisis Has Already Left Too Many Children Hungry in America." In *The Reference Shelf: Food Insecurity & Hunger in the United States,* edited by Micah L. Issitt, 82-85. Amenia, NY: Grey House Publishing, 2021.

MLA: Bauer, Lauren. "The COVID-19 Crisis Has Already Left Too Many Children Hungry in America." *The Reference Shelf: Food Insecurity & Hunger in the United States,* edited by Micah L. Issitt, Grey House Publishing, 2021, pp. 82-85.

APA: Bauer, L. (2021). The COVID-19 crisis has already left too many children hungry in America. In Micah L. Issitt (Ed.), *The reference shelf: Food insecurity & hunger in the United States* (pp. 82-85). Amenia, NY: Grey House Publishing.

A Crisis Within a Crisis: Food Insecurity and COVID-19

By Michel Martin
NPR, September 27, 2020

Over the summer, like many parents, I was looking to keep my kids productive after their summer jobs and summer sports camps were canceled. Together we came up with a project we've undertaken before—collecting books that our well-read and generous neighbors were ready to hand over—and delivering them to students and families who could use something new to read.

But with schools closed, and shelters and nursing homes off limits because of the pandemic, where to bring them? A neighbor connected us with a local school board representative, who was already delivering books to schools where food that would have been served for free or at reduced cost was instead packed up for families to pick up and eat at home. He invited us to add our contributions. After a couple of weeks of collecting, we packed up several cars with boxes and set out for our first drop.

What we saw was, well, it was shocking. We set out for our deliveries. At one school, the line for food literally wrapped around the building.

There were all kinds of folks. As you might imagine, families of school aged children, but also seniors, families of several generations and people of every possible race. Some were chatty and smiling and

> **At one school, the line for food literally wrapped around the building.**

playful with their kids and the food service folks who tried to keep the mood light, but others looked worn, tired and anxious. We'd see the same thing over and over again.

Over the course of covering the global health crisis that began earlier this year, I have heard many worries from people across the country: about getting sick, losing a job or a business, losing health insurance, depleting savings. But not until I saw people standing in line for food did it strike me that at the most basic level, all these could lead to the same thing: being hungry, or at least, not having enough food, or the right kind of food, when you need it.

I wanted to find out how that could be, so my colleagues and I decided to dedicate a special episode of *All Things Considered* to the issue of food insecurity in

America, and what people around the country are trying to do about it now, what they were doing before the coronavirus crisis and what they'll be doing after it ends.

In this episode, which you can listen to at the audio link above, we speak to Eugene Cho, CEO of Bread for the World, about what food insecurity looks like in the U.S. and how that compares to the rest of the world. We visit a food distribution center in suburban Washington, D.C., for an on-the-ground look at the issue, and hear from reporters in Illinois in Nebraska about how food insecurity is playing out in rural America. We talk to experts about how the social safety net is holding up, and look ahead with Ertharin Cousin, the founder and CEO of Food Systems for the Future.

We realize this is a global phenomenon but, sometimes, it's best to figure out what's going on around the block before you widen your lens to the rest of the world.

Print Citations

CMS: Martin, Michel. "A Crisis Within a Crisis: Food Insecurity and COVID-19." In *The Reference Shelf: Food Insecurity & Hunger in the United States,* edited by Micah L. Issitt, 86-87. Amenia, NY: Grey House Publishing, 2021.

MLA: Martin, Michel. "A Crisis Within a Crisis: Food Insecurity and COVID-19." *The Reference Shelf: Food Insecurity & Hunger in the United States,* edited by Micah L. Issitt, Grey House Publishing, 2021, pp. 86-87.

APA: Martin, M. (2021). A crisis within a crisis: Food insecurity and COVID-19. In Micah L. Issitt (Ed.), *The reference shelf: Food insecurity & hunger in the United States* (pp. 86-87). Amenia, NY: Grey House Publishing.

Study: 29 Million American Adults Don't Have Enough to Eat—Nearly a Threefold Increase from Two Years

By Sam Bloch
The Counter, September 15, 2020

Months into the pandemic, an American hunger crisis has exploded, with tens of millions of people suddenly wondering if they will be able to put food on the table.

According to a new report commissioned by the Food Research and Action Center (FRAC), as of July, the number of people who said they sometimes or often did not have enough to eat has skyrocketed to 29 million, or 11 percent of adults in the United States. (By comparison, 8 million adults, or around 4 percent, did not have enough to eat in 2018.) In 38 states and Washington, D.C., more than one in ten adults with children had inadequate amounts of food, with the highest rates of hunger in Mississippi, Louisiana, and Texas.

As expected, people of color and those without a college education were more likely to go hungry. The pandemic has exacerbated their vulnerabilities: More than 20 percent of Black and Latinx families reported they did not have enough to eat, which is double the rate of whites. Women, who were more likely to have lost their jobs, also reported higher rates of hunger.

Now, new data from the Census Bureau, referenced in the report, shows that even America's middle class is now reckoning with hunger. Two years ago, only 3 percent of adults earning between $50,000 and $75,000 a year said they did not have enough to eat; during the pandemic, that rose to 8 percent. Similarly, 5 percent of adults earning between $35,000 and $50,000 reported that hunger in 2018; now, it is 12 percent.

"These are folks who had fairly steady incomes. And now, all of a sudden, they're visiting food banks."

Among those who did not have enough to eat overall, one in four have usual incomes above $50,000 a year. Since April, millions of Americans have sought outside food assistance for the first time.

"These are folks who had fairly steady incomes," says Luis Giardia, president of FRAC, a Washington, D.C.-based nonprofit. "And now, all of a sudden, they're visiting food banks."

The analysis, conducted by Northwestern University economist Diane Schanzenbach, is based on Census Bureau data recorded between April and July. The data captures a narrower, more severe definition of hunger than the typical measure used by the United States Department of Agriculture (USDA), which is food insecurity. That term reflects a range of hardships, including not having enough money for groceries, or changing eating patterns to make up for a lack of resources. This year, an estimated 54 million people in the U.S. will be food insecure, which represents a massive leap from 35 million people in 2019.

As part of their questions, though, Census takers ask respondents if they are experiencing severe food insecurity, which means they sometimes or often go without enough food to eat. Those rates have jumped during past recessions. The share of Census respondents without enough to eat during the Great Recession, for instance, increased

> **An estimated 54 million people in the U.S. will be food insecure, which represents a massive leap from 35 million people in 2019.**

by one-third compared to the year prior. But the pandemic has caused a massive spike: The nearly threefold increase is due to record unemployment rates, and compounded by the widespread closures of schools and child care centers that normally provide meals. T

This year, an estimated 54 million people in the U.S. will be food insecure, which represents a massive leap from 35 million people in 2019.

Before the pandemic, there were already stark disparities among ethnic groups, with Black people surveyed more than three times as likely as white and Asian respondents to go hungry. But the Census data reveals that those rates have worsened. During the pandemic, 42 percent of those without enough to eat are white, followed by 27 percent Latinx, 22 percent Black, and 3 percent Asian—statistics that show Black and Latinx people of color are disproportionately affected, based on their representation within the U.S. population. The rates of hunger have quadrupled among Latinx respondents since 2018.

FRAC attributes those rates to job losses in hospitality and travel sectors, and heavy job losses among women. According to Census data, 21 percent of those who lost their jobs during the pandemic reported hunger, sometimes or often. Besides the unemployed, others have been pushed to the edge due to reduced hours. Thirteen percent of those who are still working, but have lost income, or expect to in the future, report not having enough to eat.

"What is being exposed here, number one, is that hunger and food insecurity have become a fixture of our society."

As minivans inch through parking lots, and bread lines snake around city blocks, food banks and charities are not equipped to handle the need of millions of newly famished Americans. Guardia, the FRAC president, urges federal legislators to expand policies that help the hungry, including increasing Supplemental Nutrition Assistance Program (SNAP) benefits by 15 percent, and extending Pandemic

Electronic Benefit Transfer (P-EBT) payments, which are given to families who lost access to free or reduce-priced school meals when cafeterias closed. Payments from the program have lifted as many as 3.9 million children out of hunger since the pandemic, the report claims.

Although those measures are important, they paper over a larger issue, says Alison Cohen, a program director at WhyHunger, a New York City-based nonprofit. Before the pandemic, 46 million Americans relied on food banks, and 50 percent of them either received SNAP benefits or had a family member with a full-time job, she says. Ending decades of persistent hunger in America can be achieved by enshrining a right to food, or lifting more people out of poverty with a living wage.

"What is being exposed here, number one, is that hunger and food insecurity have become a fixture of our society," Cohen said. "We have got to recognize that there were cracks in the ceiling already."

Print Citations

CMS: Bloch, Sam. "Study: 29 Million American Adults Don't Have Enough to Eat—Nearly a Threefold Increase from Two Years." In *The Reference Shelf: Food Insecurity & Hunger in the United States,* edited by Micah L. Issitt, 88-90. Amenia, NY: Grey House Publishing, 2021.

MLA: Bloch, Sam. "Study: 29 Million American Adults Don't Have Enough to Eat—Nearly a Threefold Increase from Two Years." *The Reference Shelf: Food Insecurity & Hunger in the United States,* edited by Micah L. Issitt, Grey House Publishing, 2021, pp. 88-90.

APA: Bloch, S. (2021). Study: 29 million American adults don't have enough to eat—nearly a threefold increase from two years. In Micah L. Issitt (Ed.), *The reference shelf: Food insecurity & hunger in the United States* (pp. 88-90). Amenia, NY: Grey House Publishing.

Covid-19 Pandemic Is the First Time 40% of Americans Have Experienced Food Insecurity

By Megan Leonhardt
CNBC, November 19, 2020

Monica Wahlberg has been submitting unemployment claims for the last 14 weeks, but she hasn't seen a cent yet.

After losing her dream job as the director of a Madison, Wisconsin, community arts center in June, Wahlberg was able to carry on for a while without unemployment benefits, thanks to a severance package and her savings. Wahlberg, 45, held out hope that she would be able to find another job in her field, especially since she was asked to do phone and video interviews for a range of potential employers.

But just getting by became more and more challenging as the months dragged on and her pantry supplies dried up along with her savings. After her church sponsored a pop-up food pantry over the summer, her pastor finally asked if she needed some of the leftover supplies. "I appreciated that. I realized I hadn't had any of these canned goods for a while," Wahlberg says.

Wahlberg isn't alone. About 4 in 10 Americans report that they experienced food insecurity for the first time during the Covid-19 pandemic, according to a new poll of 2,000 U.S. adults released Tuesday by Two Good Yogurt and conducted by market research company OnePoll.

About half of those polled say they've struggled to afford food, while 37% report skipping meals themselves so there was enough food for their children to eat. Yet 63% said they didn't realize they were experiencing food insecurity, which is generally defined as when an individual doesn't have reliable access to a sufficient quantity of affordable food.

The majority of Americans experiencing food insecurity, about 60%, say the expiration of many federal assistance programs, such as enhanced unemployment benefits and stimulus payments, has made it even more difficult. About half report that they're struggling to provide food for their families more now than they were at the beginning of the pandemic.

Demand Hasn't Stopped

Food insecurity didn't start with the pandemic, but the crisis did exacerbate existing problems.

Prior to the start of the pandemic in March, about 35 million Americans—including approximately 11 million children—lived in households that were food insecure, according to Feeding America, a leading national nonprofit food bank network. That was the lowest food insecurity rate the U.S. had seen in 20 years.

If the unemployment rate averages 10.5% this year and the poverty rate comes in above 14%, which Feeding America expects the U.S. to hit, more than 50 million people will experience food insecurity, including about 17 million children, the organization estimates. The U.S. unemployment rate rose to a record high of 14.7% in April, according to the Bureau of Labor Statistics.

37% report skipping meals themselves so there was enough food for their children to eat.

Federal programs such as the Supplemental Nutrition Assistance Program (SNAP), the Special Supplemental Nutrition Program for Women, Infants and Children (WIC) and the Emergency Food Assistance Program (TEFAP) are helping, but food banks and pantries are picking up a lot of the slack. Food banks have been experiencing ballooning demand for months now, which may not be sustainable long-term.

"The problem hasn't gone away," says Laura Lester, director of the Alabama Food Bank Association. "The initial crushing blow of everything has eased up a little, but not as much as you would think."

The high level of demand comes at a cost, Lester says. Her network of food banks has started discussing the "inevitable food cliff." When that happens, food banks may need to limit their services.

That's because food banks are generally responsible for sourcing, storing and delivering supplies to local food pantries. Typically, they'd rely on donated food to supply the majority of their provisions, but that's not enough to keep up now. As a result, food banks are buying more food than ever before to meet the demand.

New York-based City Harvest spent about $10 million on food purchases from March through November. That's up nearly 50 times the $208,000 the organization typically spends in a normal fiscal year.

City Harvest expects that number to continue to rise, says CEO Jilly Stephens. The organization predicts that demand will rise dramatically in January since more federal programs are set to expire at the end of the year, including the Farmers to Families Food Boxes and the Pandemic Unemployment Assistance.

"We don't see the numbers diminishing," Stephens says, especially as things get harder. "When the days get colder and shorter, people need that food."

Plus, it can take people a while to turn to emergency food. Like Wahlberg, there may be many Americans who are struggling right now, but haven't yet turned to food assistance programs or pantries because they're first maxing out their credit cards or spending down their savings.

"Many people will exhaust all sorts of resources before they go and stand in line for food," Stephens says.

Getting the Help You Need

Yet perhaps more troubling than food banks' expected shortages is the fact that many people who are grappling with hunger don't know how to get the assistance they need. Nearly 4 out of 5 survey respondents say they struggled to find the support they needed.

Wahlberg was no different. Although she accepted the leftovers from her church's pop-up food pantry, she didn't start to regularly use food pantries until a few months later.

Through a local program focused on workers displaced by the pandemic, Wahlberg received a six-week, part-time job making $15 an hour at Madison-based The River Food Pantry. It was only after she joined The River that she started to regularly make use of their food assistance services.

Initially, though, she'd help didn't grab anything for herself, even though she was struggling. "They asked me, have you picked up food? And I was like, 'No, but I'd like to,'" Wahlberg says. When she did, Wahlberg says there was no judgement or issues.

"There is a stigma of, 'I volunteer and I donate—I don't use these services.' But that really needs to be broken down," Wahlberg says. Working at a food pantry and being a client is what's keeping her afloat right now.

"If I had to spend my own money on food, then that's money I have to cut from my heating bill or my Internet or my telephone," she says. While phone service and Internet may seem like luxuries, she needs those things to apply for jobs, she says.

Although her six weeks with the job placement program recently expired, Wahlberg says the pantry decided to keep her on through the end of the year working 10 hours a week. "I still don't have a [full-time] job and I'm literally living off of my paycheck from The River," Wahlberg says.

But she's quick to point out that she's fortunate to have that paycheck, as well as support from family and friends who have been able to help her out this year. From a board member for her condo association who used their stimulus check to pay Wahlberg's dues for a few months to friends who send her checks in the mail every once in a while, she's able to get by.

"I'm doing OK, but it's through the grace of God and the generosity of my network," she says.

Print Citations

CMS: Leonhardt, Megan. "Covid-19 Pandemic Is the First Time 40% of Americans Have Experienced Food Insecurity." In *The Reference Shelf: Food Insecurity & Hunger in the United States,* edited by Micah L. Issitt, 91-94. Amenia, NY: Grey House Publishing, 2021.

MLA: Leonhardt, Megan. "Covid-19 Pandemic Is the First Time 40% of Americans Have Experienced Food Insecurity." *The Reference Shelf: Food Insecurity & Hunger in the United States,* edited by Micah L. Issitt, Grey House Publishing, 2021, pp. 91-94.

APA: Leonhardt, M. (2021). Covid-19 pandemic is the first time 40% of Americans have experienced food insecurity. In Micah L. Issitt (Ed.), *The reference shelf: Food insecurity & hunger in the United States* (pp. 91-94). Amenia, NY: Grey House Publishing.

4

The World's Problem

By Bob Nichols, USDA, via Wikimedia.

A Texas cornfield impacted by severe drought, a byproduct of climate change.

Global Factors Contributing to Hunger

The interconnectedness of the modern world means that there are few major issues that affect just one country. This is especially true for countries like the United States, which has never truly been independent and isolated from the rest of the world. The United States began as a globalist endeavor, with Europe seeking to gain an advantage in the global trade for spices and other food resources, and the nation has remained closely linked to global trade partners ever since. Nearly 1 out of every 5 Americans is employed in jobs that would not exist without foreign trade, and the $5.6 trillion in trade outside of the United States props up the entire economy. Any change in the global economy has the potential to impact people living in the United States, and the strength of the U.S. economy is linked to the strength of the global economy.[1]

The U.S. food industry is also heavily dependent on foreign trade. In total, around 15 percent of all food consumed in the United States is imported, and this includes over 50 percent of all fruit and more than 30 percent of vegetables, which constitutes much of the healthy food in American supermarkets.[2] Foreign trade agreements and the strength of foreign economies thereby play a major role in determining the cost of food in the United States, and this impacts hunger and food insecurity. The efforts of legislators and activists to reform the U.S. economy and food industry to protect consumers cannot succeed without some consideration of how U.S. imports and exports impact food prices and availability.

There is another way in which the interconnectedness of the world makes hunger and poverty global issues: all nations depend on the resources of a single planet. The availability of those resources depends on whether or not countries engage in sustainable resource development and on the state of the global climate and environment. Millions around the world face hunger because of climate change and its effect on agriculture. As the climate continues to change, leading to more frequent and prolonged resource shortages, military and diplomatic conflicts are more likely to emerge, potentially impacting the global economy. In the twenty-first century, the world has seen numerous military conflicts, like the ongoing civil war in the Sudan, that are directly the result of climate change creating shortages in food and water and leading to violence. As climate change limits agricultural productivity, this can increase food costs and reduce availability. This affects America's global agricultural commodities, both in terms of imports and exports, but also impacts the domestic agricultural industry.

A Dependent Economy

The welfare of the American people is, in many ways, impacted by the health of the global economy and America's involvement in foreign economic systems. For instance, in the United States, politicians and economic analysts have long be-moaned that the nation is heavily dependent on foreign oil. This dependence has come with a significant cost. The United States has been involved in wars, fraught diplomatic conflicts, and has engaged in colonialist military aggression, for the sake of maintaining the nation's oil supplies.[3] The effort to maintain access to foreign oil not only plays a dominant role in shaping American foreign policy, but also impacts the entire national economy as the cost of oil is a major factor in household finances as well. Likewise, the cost of gasoline figures into whether or not individuals can af-ford to travel greater distances to obtain food, and also impacts the cost of process-ing, storing, and distributing food throughout the country. Moreover, because the fossil fuel industry is the number one driver of climate change, U.S. involvement in the foreign oil market is contributing to environmental changes that are ultimately contributing to agricultural decline and so increasing food costs in America and contributing to the problems of hunger and poverty.

One of the issues emerging from the global food economy is the idea of "food security," which refers to whether a population has reliable access to affordable and nutritious food. Food security is often discussed as if it is a local or at least domestic issue, but in reality there are strong links between food security in the United States and the global economy. The United States can never achieve full food security, for instance, without considering the contributions of other nations to the U.S. food supply. Global distribution systems, foreign trade and diplomatic agreements, and complex global financial relationships also play a major role in determining what kinds of food will be available to U.S. consumers, as well as how much food will cost. This is true not only for imported foods, but also for domestic foods because the strength of America's international financial connections can determine the cost of domestic goods as well, through its influence on taxation, the cost of oil, the cost of labor, etc.

While the relationship between the global economy and hunger in America is complex, there are several factors that stand out as important features. Specula-tion on commodities—the way in which investors essentially bet on increases or decreases in food prices—can impact supply and demand systems for various com-modities. This, in turn, can have a dramatic impact on nations depending on im-porting or exporting certain food products. Restrictions on imports and exports, tar-iffs, and other trade policies likewise impact hunger and food security by causing prices to fluctuate. Further, the nations of the world have created a system that con-tributes to uneven investment in agriculture. Products sought by those in wealthy countries are produced in abundance, which keeps costs low but also limits food security by creating populations of agricultural workers dependent on just a few crops. The United States subsidizes agricultural workers to compensate for fluctua-tions in supply and demand, but many nations cannot do this. Agricultural workers in many poorer nations are highly dependent on continued demand. Something as simple as a "food trend" among affluent Americans can have a dramatic impact on small farming communities in other nations. When a trendy food falls out of favor, thousands can fall into destitution.[4]

Some Americans also see global food market instability and global hunger as important issues from a human rights perspective. Global hunger is a major humanitarian issue, with more than 800 million around the world either undernourished or malnourished and many in developing economies living in or below poverty, with little access to nutritious food. America's role in the global economy and the global trade in agricultural products can play a major role in global hunger and poverty. It is an important goal to shape U.S. foreign policies whenever possible to alleviate global humanitarian issues.[5]

The Changing World

Another major factor impacting global hunger is climate change. Scientists working around the world have gathered sufficient data to prove that that the average temperature of the world is increasing, and that this will have a devastating impact on every population. Climate change is now considered the single greatest driver of global hunger, and it is accelerating over time.

Extreme weather events, like tornadoes, tsunamis, floods, and droughts, can decimate agricultural regions and communities. Climate change not only causes more extreme high temperatures during hot or dry seasons but also causes extreme temperature drops during the winter and can cause extreme rainfall during wet seasons. As the average temperature climbs, familiar weather patterns are thrown into chaos and, over time, this leads to unpredictable weather patterns and makes it difficult for agricultural communities to adjust. Over the past 30 years, extreme weather events have doubled in frequency and increased in intensity. The Atlantic hurricane season has been increasingly destructive and prolonged over the past decades, leading to a major humanitarian and economic crisis in the United States. Similar patterns are occurring around the world, leading to a reduction in agricultural productivity and the loss of key agricultural crops in areas dependent on agriculture for survival.[6]

Further, nearly a third of the world's arable land has already been degraded to the point of losing productivity. This trend will accelerate as increased heat and frequent droughts further deteriorate remaining farmable territory around the world. As temperatures rise, deserts and other arid landscapes will increase in size. Deciduous forests, scrub land, and fertile prairies will decrease. The loss of farmable land isn't only a matter of climate change and also involves factors such as industrial pollution, erosion, and unsustainable agricultural practices, but climate change will accelerate this process. As arable land is diminished, many more communities will face food shortages, increased hunger, and diminished food security. The loss of farmland also comes as the demand for food is increasing exponentially due to unchecked population growth.[7]

Perhaps the most direct impact of climate change on hunger will be seen in water shortages. There are parts of the United States in which residents are frequently asked to ration water use to avoid running out of minimum supplies. This problem is increasing due to lower levels of annual rainfall and higher average temperatures. Water shortages also lead to limited agricultural productivity, and the threat of prolonged draught contributes to food and job insecurity for many agricultural workers and consumers around the United States. This problem is most severe in areas with arid or semi-arid climates, where water shortages are part of the natural cycle. However, with water shortages becoming more frequent and lasting longer, agricultural production in many regions is under threat, and coming years may well see an unsustainable decline in productivity.[8]

Humans have been aware of climate change for decades and the failure of the global population to adjust to this potentially devastating reality reflects the dominance of the fossil fuel industry and their fight to preserve their profit. Fossil fuel lobbyists and allied politicians have repeatedly misinformed consumers around the world, denying the severity of the climate change problem and even producing illegitimate scientific studies to call the scientific consensus on climate change into question.

Unforeseen Factors

The most pressing unforeseen factor in the 2020s is the COVID-19 crisis. The spread of the deadly COVID-19 disease disrupted global economies and livelihoods. Supplies of certain food products dwindled, and the patterns of supply and demand shifted, throwing the global food market into turmoil. Ultimately, the COVID-19 pandemic led to a major surge in unemployment, and this increased poverty rates and also led to the growth of the population struggling with food insecurity.

As is typically the case, when global society is thrown into disarray, the poor and vulnerable are the first to suffer and suffer the most lasting impact. Though it has been a scramble for global society to adjust to the rapid emergence and spread of the pandemic, social welfare organizations have struggled to adjust to the way that the pandemic impacted disadvantaged communities and individuals. The United Nation's World Food Program won the 2020 Nobel Peace Prize for quickly enhancing the organization's efforts to combat global food insecurity during the pandemic. Conducting research and funding important grassroots efforts to combat hunger, the World Food Program issued a statement that the population facing food insecurity is likely to double in 2020, from 135 million to more than 265 million. Climate and other factors were also linked to the increase in food insecurity, but COVID-19 was considered one of the driving factors.[9]

The Interconnected World

The modern world is one of increasing interconnectedness and so every decision, even at the local, community level, can have a collective global impact. Solving major global crises like the food and hunger crisis requires not only local action, but also must consider the broader global patterns that undergird food insecurity. Only by tackling the problems within and outside of the nation, can Americans make significant progress in ending hunger and increasing food security for the American people.

Works Used

Bordoff, Jason. "The Myth of U.S. Energy Independence Has Gone Up in Smoke." *FP. Foreign Policy.* Sep 18, 2019. https://foreignpolicy.com/2019/09/18/the-myth-of-u-s-energy-independence-has-gone-up-in-smoke/.

Clapp, Jennifer. "World Hunger and the Global Economy: Strong Linkages, Weak Action." *Journal of International Affairs*, vol. 67, no. 2, 2014. https://core.ac.uk/download/pdf/144150286.pdf.

Karp, David. "Most of America's Fruit Is Now Imported: Is That a Bad Thing?" *New York Times.* Mar 13, 2018. https://www.nytimes.com/2018/03/13/dining/fruit-vegetables-imports.html.

Kretchmer, Harry. "Global Hunger Fell for Decades, but It's Rising Again." *We Forum.* Jul 23, 2020. https://www.weforum.org/agenda/2020/07/global-hunger-rising-food-agriculture-organization-rport/.

Milman, Oliver. "Earth Has Lost a Third of Arable Land in Past 40 Years, Scientists Say." *The Guardian.* Dec 2, 2015. https://www.theguardian.com/environment/2015/dec/02/arable-land-soil-food-security-shortage.

"New Data Confirm Increased Frequency of Extreme Weather Events." *Science Daily.* Mar 21, 2018. https://www.sciencedaily.com/releases/2018/03/180321130859.htm.

"New Study: International Trade Supports Nearly 39 Million American Jobs." *Business Roundtable.* Mar 18, 2019. https://www.businessroundtable.org/new-study-international-trade-supports-nearly-39-million-american-jobs.

Nugent, Ciara. "The World Food Programme Won the 2020 Nobel Peace Prize: Here's How the Pandemic Has Made Its Work Even More Essential." *Time.* Oct 9, 2020. https://time.com/5898641/nobel-peace-prize-covid-19-hunger-crisis/.

"UN Warns Climate Change Is Driving Global Hunger," *UNFCCC.* Sep 12, 2018. https://unfccc.int/news/un-warns-climate-change-is-driving-global-hunger.

Notes

1. "New Study: International Trade Supports Nearly 39 Million American Jobs," *Business Roundtable.*
2. Karp, "Most of America's Fruit Is Now Imported: Is That a Bad Thing?"
3. Bordoff, "The Myth of U.S. Energy Independence Has Gond Up in Smoke."
4. Clapp, "World Hunger and the Global Economy: Strong Linkages, Weak Action."
5. Kretchmer, "Global Hunger Fell for Decades, but It's Rising Again."
6. "New Data Confirm Increased Frequency of Extreme Weather Events," *Science Daily.*
7. Milman, "Earth Has Lost a Third of Arable Land in Past 40 Years, Scientists Say."
8. "UN Warns Climate Change Is Driving Global Hunger," *UNFCCC.*
9. Nugent, "The World Food Programme Won the 2020 Nobel Peace Prize: Here's How the Pandemic Has Made Its Work Even More Essential."

Climate Change and Global Hunger

By Emily Folk
Ecologist, August 21, 2020

Hunger remains a global crisis. Around the world, 135 million people in 55 countries face acute hunger every year.

New research on the links between climate change and food security suggests this crisis may soon become even worse.

Natural disasters, which scientists believe may have been made worse or more frequent by climate change, are doing more damage than usual to global food production systems.

Disasters

As a result, this phenomenon is majorly impacting almost every aspect of agriculture and food distribution.

More intense floods and droughts can destroy harvests, driving up food prices and limiting the variety of food available.

This article shows how climate change is making hunger worse in some of the world's poorest countries—and what governments can do to mitigate the effects.

As the planet warms, extreme weather events are becoming more common and more severe. Droughts, floods and other extreme weather events damage infrastructure and housing—as well as agriculture.

The most food-insecure countries—which are also those that generate the least amount of greenhouse gas emissions—are already feeling the impacts of these increasingly severe disasters.

Ambitious

Floods, made worse by climate change, can destroy crops, cause landslides and strip away topsoil.

At the same time, increased heat appears to be making disease outbreaks in livestock and crops more common.

In recent years, fish yields from Lake Tanganyika have fallen dramatically, and scientists believe the lake's rapidly warming waters may be partly to blame.

Current research shows that as temperatures rise, crop production will get more and more difficult. According to one study, corn yields will decrease an average of 7.4 percent for every degree Celsius of warming.

Worldwide, the most ambitious climate change policies look to limit warming to two degrees Celsius.

Nutraceuticals

However, not every government is taking enough action to meet these goals. In the worst-case scenario, we may be on track for as much as four degrees of warming.

This level of warming would have a devastating impact on food production around the globe—especially in those regions that already struggle to manage food insecurity.

In the near term, new agricultural practices could help curb agriculture's environmental impact and improve nutrition in food-insecure regions.

According to the UN's Food and Agricultural Organization, for example, the cultivation of edible insects in place of conventional livestock could significantly decrease agricultural emissions.

Increased cultivation of nutritionally dense foods, like nutraceuticals, could also help prevent malnutrition and nutritional deficiencies in food-stressed areas.

Malnutrition

At the same time, regenerative agriculture practices could help rebuild topsoil and restore fish stocks in areas struck by landslides and warming waters.

Building resilience to climate change in communities that are most likely to be impacted could also help.

For example, programs that help countries detect the early signs of food insecurity may improve their ability to mount quick responses to food production failures.

Quick responses to malnutrition are typically much cheaper and more effective than late ones.

During the early days of the 2005 Niger famine, for example, it would have cost $1 a day per child to prevent acute malnutrition if early warning signs had been acknowledged.

> **Increased cultivation of nutritionally dense foods, like nutraceuticals, could also help prevent malnutrition and nutritional deficiencies in food-stressed areas.**

Droughts

By July 2006, the cost of emergency operations had increased to $80 per malnourished child.

According to analysis from ACF International, early warning systems exist in many countries vulnerable to food insecurity, but these systems are often underdeveloped.

Investing in these programs could help countries quickly and more effectively respond to malnutrition.

So long as temperatures continue to rise, climate change-related food insecurity will remain a major issue for countries around the globe.

Floods, droughts and warming waters will have major impacts on food production, both in the short- and long-term.

Agriculture

Quick action can help food-insecure countries manage the impact of climate change. New agricultural practices, like the cultivation of low-emission livestock and nutrient-dense foods, may also help these nations improve their climate change resiliency.

The best long-term strategy, however, will need to include programs that curb global greenhouse gas emissions. Even a 2-degree Celsius change in temperature will have a major influence on the production of staple crops.

More ambitious climate action would almost certainly help prevent malnutrition that comes from falling crop yields as temperatures rise.

Programs that look to combat malnutrition, like the Scaling Up Nutrition movement, will also continue to be essential.

Ending or reducing malnutrition where it exists right now will help those communities better manage the future effects of climate change on agriculture.

Print Citations

CMS: Folk, Emily. "Climate Change and Global Hunger." In *The Reference Shelf: Food Insecurity & Hunger in the United States,* edited by Micah L. Issitt, 103-105. Amenia, NY: Grey House Publishing, 2021.

MLA: Folk, Emily. "Climate Change and Global Hunger." *The Reference Shelf: Food Insecurity & Hunger in the United States,* edited by Micah L. Issitt, Grey House Publishing, 2021, pp. 103-105.

APA: Folk, E. (2021). Climate change and global hunger. In Micah L. Issitt (Ed.), *The reference shelf: Food insecurity & hunger in the United States* (pp. 103-105). Amenia, NY: Grey House Publishing.

World Hunger Has Risen for Three Straight Years, and Climate Change Is a Cause

By Jessica Eise and Kenneth Foster
The Conversation, October 22, 2018

World hunger has risen for a third consecutive year, according to the United Nations' annual food security report. The total number of people who face chronic food deprivation has increased by 15 million since 2016. Some 821 million people now face food insecurity, raising numbers to the same level as almost a decade ago.

The situation is worsening in South America, Central Asia and most regions of Africa, the report shows. It also spotlights a troubling rise in anemia among women of reproductive age. One in 3 women worldwide are affected, with health and developmental consequences for them and their children.

From 2005 to 2014, global undernourishment was on the decline. But the rate of decline continuously eroded, like a car moving forward at an ever-decreasing speed. Several years ago it stopped altogether, and world hunger started to climb once more. Among the factors driving this reversal was climate change.

While malnutrition and food insecurity begin at the household level, hunger is everyone's business. The damage wrought by hunger on communities can provoke regional instability and conflict that can extend beyond impacted areas. For example, drought and crop failures in Central America are among the drivers of immigration across the U.S. border.

Climate, Weather, and Crops

The causes of food insecurity are complex and interrelated. In our recent book, *How to Feed the World*, a collection of essays from leading researchers, we review pressing challenges. Among them, climate change emerges as a troubling problem that influences all others.

Earth's climate has swung into and out of ice ages since the dawn of time. In the last 50 years, however, things have changed. Average global temperatures have increased ever more quickly, with new recorded highs in 2014, then again in 2015, and again in 2016.

Climate change is also increasing the severity and frequency of extreme weather events, such as powerful storms and droughts. As a result, some regions of the world are getting wetter, including the northern United States and Canada, while others are becoming drier, such as the southwestern United States. In the U.S. Midwest, heavy rainfalls events increased by over a third from 1958 to 2012.

Climate change is anticipated to force more than 100 million people into extreme poverty by 2030.

Agriculture is one of the industries that is most exposed and vulnerable to climate change. Crops and livestock are extremely sensitive to temperature and precipitation. A late spring frost can be devastating, and a heat wave during the flowering stage can result in sharply reduced yields. In short, agriculture is the "Goldilocks industry." The weather should not be too hot or too cold, and rainfall must be "just right."

Producing enough food for everyone in the world depends heavily on climate. This means that it will be impossible to curb hunger without preparing for and adapting to climate change.

The Importance of Agricultural Research

Climate change renders generational and historical information about farming less valuable. What worked before may no longer apply in an altered climate. When historical knowledge no longer works, farmers must rely on other sources of information, such as meteorologists, agronomists and other scientists, as well as the development of new sustainable technologies.

Farmers in the most advanced economies, including the United States, already rely heavily on scientific knowledge, which is often mediated by the private sector or by local extension services. However, farmers in the poorest countries—which in many cases will suffer the most severe impacts from climate change—rarely have access to such knowledge.

Even in wealthy countries, these adjustments are costly. And public funding for agricultural research and development has been declining for a decade in the United States. The poorest countries in the world account for just 3 percent of global spending on agricultural research. Without investments into sharing research discoveries, many advances in wealthier countries will not be transferred to low-income nations.

Climate Change's Pervasive Influence

Climate change also intensifies other stresses on global food production. Consider the critical role of water. Meat consumption alone accounts for an estimated 22 percent of global water use, and this need will increase in a hotter world. Climate change also alters rainfall patterns: Some places will have too little water to farm, while others may have enough but find that it falls at the wrong time, or arrives less frequently but in larger rainfall events.

Even seemingly disparate factors like international trade are affected by climate change, with serious ramifications for food security. As climate change drives permanent shifts in the geography of world agricultural production zones, international trade will emerge as an important resiliency mechanism for reducing hunger and for enhancing equal access to food.

For instance, a 2012 heat wave and drought prompted major losses in corn harvests in the United States. Producers in the Southern Hemisphere adjusted to the shortfall, which served to moderate price increases in the United States. This was only possible because of international trade.

An effective response to climate change will also be critical to making progress on a host of other food security challenges, such as curbing food loss, improving nutrition and promoting sustainable production systems. Food-producing nations will need creative policies and new technologies to meet these challenges successfully.

Adapting to New Conditions

Climate change is anticipated to force more than 100 million people into extreme poverty by 2030. Adapting to climate change is a key way to combat this–and technology can help.

For instance, precision agriculture can leverage computers, global positioning systems, geographic information systems and sensors to provide the data necessary to give each tiny parcel of land on a field exactly the inputs it needs. And a resurgent interest is occurring in use of the time-honored technology of cover crops to mitigate climate change impacts.

We can go even smaller in our measurements with the emergence of nanotechnology. Aside from making field sensors smaller and more compact, nanotechnologies can also help improve how fertilizers and pesticides are released. By putting chemical inputs into tiny capsules or in gels, it is possible to control when and how these inputs are released to make them more effective, and at the same time reduce chemical emissions and runoff.

But ultimately, it is up to individuals. Around the world, people must wield their social power to encourage mitigation of climate change and promote investments in technologies for adaptation. We need everyone at the table contributing to a food-secure future.

Print Citations

CMS: Eise, Jessica, and Kenneth Foster. "World Hunger Has Risen for Three Straight Years, and Climate Change Is a Cause." In *The Reference Shelf: Food Insecurity & Hunger in the United States,* edited by Micah L. Issitt, 106-108. Amenia, NY: Grey House Publishing, 2021.

MLA: Eise, Jessica, and Kenneth Foster. "World Hunger Has Risen for Three Straight Years, and Climate Change Is a Cause." *The Reference Shelf: Food Insecurity & Hunger in the United States,* edited by Micah L. Issitt, Grey House Publishing, 2021, pp. 106-108.

APA: Eise, J., & Foster, K. (2021). World hunger has risen for three straight years, and climate change is a cause. In Micah L. Issitt (Ed.), *The reference shelf: Food insecurity & hunger in the United States* (pp. 106-108). Amenia, NY: Grey House Publishing.

Trump's Trade Wars Have Made Bad Agriculture Policies Worse

By Clark Packard
Foreign Policy, October 27, 2020

Recent years have been tumultuous for American farmers and ranchers. Thanks to advanced technologies and generous subsidies, their products have become so abundant that the United States usually ends up exporting about 20 percent of its agricultural output abroad. To keep growing, U.S. farmers and ranchers need better access to markets abroad. But U.S. agriculture and trade policies run counter to the more liberalized and open markets that would benefit U.S. farmers. These obstacles didn't originate with President Donald Trump. He's raised them higher, to be sure, but only within a system that was already deeply flawed.

One of Trump's first actions as president was to make good on a campaign pledge to withdraw the United States from the Trans-Pacific Partnership (TPP), a promising free-trade agreement with Pacific Rim nations signed in early 2016. No one would have gained more from the TPP than U.S. farmers and ranchers, who would have seen significantly improved access to the notoriously closed agricultural markets of Asian countries such as Japan. Following the same refrain, Trump then threatened to withdraw the United States from the Clinton-era North American Free Trade Agreement (NAFTA) with Canada and Mexico, before settling on minor revisions of the 25-year-old pact.

When it comes to U.S. producers, however, the damage from Trump's actions on these agreements pales next to the damage done by his tariffs and trade wars. In early 2018, Trump invoked highly dubious national security concerns in order to slap tariffs on steel and aluminum imports from virtually every country in the world, including long-standing allies. Predictably, the United States' trading partners retaliated with their own tariffs, including on a number of U.S. agricultural products.

Trump's aggressive trade war with China took things from bad to worse for U.S. farmers. Over the course of about 18 months, Washington and Beijing engaged in a back-and-forth volley of escalating trade restrictions, including Chinese retaliatory tariffs on more than 1,000 categories of U.S. agricultural products such as pork, soybeans, dairy products, and nuts. In January 2020, the two sides signed a detente, but it's only a temporary reprieve to a conflict that continues to fester and is likely to resurface in the near future. As part of the so-called phase one agreement, Beijing agreed to purchase about $40 billion worth of U.S. agricultural products over two years, but as of September, China's agricultural purchases were barely half of what they'd need to be to reach the agreed target for 2020. Meanwhile, heavy tariffs remain in place on both sides.

With American agriculture caught in the middle of Trump's trade wars, the sector has predictably suffered. Farm bankruptcies are soaring as farmers lose market access abroad. To help mitigate the fallout from his trade wars and combat the financial toll of COVID-19, the Trump administration has shoveled tens of billions of dollars to farmers, ranchers, and companies in the sector—a key electoral constituency for Trump's reelection prospects. In 2020 alone, the Trump administration will have paid an estimated $45 billion to the agricultural sector. This has increased net farm income, which is up sharply since 2016, mainly thanks to Trump's subsidies. But the bulk of these payments went to wealthy farms and well-connected corporations while providing little relief to the neediest farmers and ranchers. It is estimated that a staggering 40 percent of the sector's income this year will come from government subsidies.

As the election nears, many are wondering about Trump's political calculus. The Office of Special Counsel recently chided Agriculture Secretary Sonny Perdue for violating federal law by using his official position to campaign for Trump, promising a North Carolina crowd in August that subsidies will continue for "four more years … if America gets out and votes for this man, Donald J. Trump."

A staggering 40 percent of the agriculture sector's income this year will come from government subsidies.

The Trump administration's aggressive foray into protectionism has been costly to farmers, but misguided agricultural policies obviously predate the trade war. Every five years in an overwhelmingly bipartisan fashion, the U.S. Congress doles out billions of dollars in subsidies to the U.S. agriculture industry in a hodgepodge of various programs. Like the Trump administration's bailouts, these policies aren't just expensive. They also largely benefit wealthy farms and corporations while failing to provide an adequate safety net for family farms. This inequity extends beyond U.S. borders: Domestic subsidies hurt farmers in developing countries who cannot compete with heavily subsidized agriculture from the wealthiest country in the world.

Despite the enormous setback for American farmers due to Trump's tariffs and trade wars, a reversal is possible. That the U.S. public has soured on foreign trade is a popular political narrative, but it's unfounded. In fact, more Americans support trade than any other time in the last quarter century. Policymakers in Washington can capitalize on this enthusiasm to expand market access for American farmers and ranchers by unwinding Trump's tariff wars and rejoining the TPP to improve access to vital Asian markets. Finally, and perhaps most critically, the United States should use its biggest bargaining chip—reining in domestic subsidies—to jumpstart multilateral negotiations at the World Trade Organization, where agricultural subsidies and tariffs have long been a major stumbling block.

Trump deserves a lot of blame for his misguided trade and agriculture policies. But many of the excesses in the U.S. system—sold to the public as a safety net for family farms but largely a system of corporate welfare for the largest producers—have a long bipartisan history. The next administration can and should do better.

Print Citations

CMS: Packard, Clark. "Trump's Trade Wars Have Made Bad Agriculture Policies Worse." In *The Reference Shelf: Food Insecurity & Hunger in the United States,* edited by Micah L. Issitt, 109-111. Amenia, NY: Grey House Publishing, 2021.

MLA: Packard, Clark. "Trump's Trade Wars Have Made Bad Agriculture Policies Worse." *The Reference Shelf: Food Insecurity & Hunger in the United States,* edited by Micah L. Issitt, Grey House Publishing, 2021, pp. 109-111.

APA: Packard, C. (2021). Trump's trade wars have made bad agriculture policies worse. In Micah L. Issitt (Ed.), *The reference shelf: Food insecurity & hunger in the United States* (pp. 109-111). Amenia, NY: Grey House Publishing.

Food Banks Win in a Trump Trade War

By April Simpson
Pew Stateline, June 4, 2019

SILVER SPRING, Md.—The shelves at your local food bank are likely stocked. Give credit to President Donald Trump's trade war with China.

Food banks have been the beneficiaries of a U.S. Department of Agriculture program crafted last year and recently extended to support farmers affected by China's retaliatory tariffs. Part of the farmer bailout includes a $1.4 billion program to buy surplus commodities affected by the trade tariffs and distribute them to food banks, schools and other outlets that serve low-income people. The purchases include beef, grapes, lentils, oranges, pistachios, pork, strawberries and tomatoes.

Leaders at food banks say the program has helped them provide their clients with healthy food, though maintaining and distributing perishable goods has come with unexpected costs. But critics say donating food to the needy is merely a beneficial side effect of the aid program and won't put a substantial dent in food waste or hunger.

"That combination of trade war and additional food for food banks is not the policy mix I would have recommended," said Parke Wilde, a food economist at the Friedman School of Nutrition Science and Policy at Tufts University in Boston. "It's better to have a fairly well functioning trade policy and less need for mitigation for food banks."

Still, food banks are happy to have the additional items, even if it means adding freezers and storage space to accommodate it.

"This food is certainly very valuable to us as an organization and specifically the fresh items have been a huge benefit," said Molly McGlinchy, senior director of procurement and direct programs for Capital Area Food Bank in Washington, D.C. "This past winter, we had a pretty tough growing season, so the fresh items that the trade mitigation offered procured a large variety of fruits and vegetables we wouldn't otherwise have been able to provide to the community."

As part of the farmer bailout, the USDA is increasing the volume of goods it distributes through its nutrition assistance programs, such as The Emergency Food Assistance Program, or TEFAP, which helps supplement the diets of low-income Americans.

Food waste occurs at every stage of the supply chain, from farmer to retailer to consumer, but most waste happens in homes, grocery stores and food service facilities. Several states distribute blemished produce, which can be difficult to sell, from farms to food banks.

But Christopher Barrett, an agricultural and development economist at the SC Johnson College of Business at Cornell University, emphasized that the food bank component of the trade aid "isn't a food waste reduction program," but rather "a farm support payments program."

Leaders of farm groups such as the American Soybean Association and the American Farm Bureau Federation, who met with Trump following the trade aid announcement, say they're pleased the administration is supporting farmers and ranchers, but that the program is only a Band-Aid. They would prefer open markets on which to sell their products.

For its part, the USDA has been clear that the trade mitigation programs are designed to help farmers, not food banks. In its first announcement of aid July 24, USDA explained that Trump directed Agriculture Secretary Sonny Perdue "to craft a relief strategy to protect agricultural producers," while the Trump administration continues to work out a trade policy that it says will help American farmers compete globally in the long run.

On May 23, the Trump administration announced a second aid package to farmers, with the bulk of the funds going to direct payments to producers. The $16 billion bailout includes a $1.4 billion "Food Purchase and Distribution Program" of surplus commodities such as fruit, vegetables, some processed foods, beef, pork,

> **Consuming food donations is known to improve the food security status of clients by increasing their intake of fruit, vegetables and proteins.**

lamb, poultry and milk, that go to food banks. An initial $12 billion farmer bailout announced last July sent 10% to the program.

As of May 20, $8.54 billion has been paid to farmers, and the Food Purchase and Distribution Program had bought $703 million of commodities, according to an email sent from the USDA press office in response to *Stateline* questions. The program is expected to continue through January 2020.

"This is a case where the administration should be praised for doing something like this," said Craig Gundersen, professor of agricultural and consumer economics at the University of Illinois at Urbana-Champaign. "I don't think it's going to have a big impact. It's a nice bonus, but when it goes away, it goes away."

Farmer Philanthropy

Meanwhile, the 2018 farm bill allocates $20 million over the next five years to establishing a farm-to-food bank initiative.

Feeding hungry people by donating extra food to food banks is high on the Environmental Protection Agency's food recovery hierarchy to prevent and divert wasted food.

About 11.8% of U.S. households were food insecure, without the resources to obtain enough food to meet their needs, in 2017, according to the USDA Economic Research Service. The proportion of food insecure households increases to 15.7% when considering only households with children. Consuming food donations is known to improve the food security status of clients by increasing their intake of fruit, vegetables and proteins.

Some states incentivize farmers to give. In 2017, after two consecutive vetoes from Democratic Gov. Andrew Cuomo, New York state enacted a tax credit for donations of agricultural products to the food recovery system. The law took effect in January 2018.

At least seven other states, (California, Colorado, Iowa, Kentucky, Missouri, Oregon and Virginia) as well as the District of Columbia offer similar credits.

It's unclear what effect the president's trade mitigation program will have on state tax incentive programs, though it might compete with programs such as the one in New York, according to David Just, behavioral economist at the SC Johnson College of Business at Cornell University.

"Farmers are very sensitive to prices and to taxes," Just said. "But my guess is that the price incentive is going to make a bigger difference to them."

Giving to the Needy

Some argue that it doesn't matter that the president's trade mitigation program wasn't created with the poor in mind. Initially, food stamps weren't created to feed the poor either, but to support the price of food during the Great Depression after a decline in crop prices created a crisis in rural America.

After World War II, American farmers created surpluses that were distributed to feed the hungry in Europe. As food aid increased, so did support for feeding the hungry at home, according to a piece in JSTOR Daily.

"This does tend to be a direct benefit for farmers in that it raises prices for their goods," Just said, "and it can dull the shock and the pain from the tariffs that are out there."

The Emergency Food Assistance Program, or TEFAP, goods on a storage rack at Shepherd's Table, a soup kitchen in Silver Spring, Maryland. The goods help supplement the diets of low-income Americans.

In the meantime, the food pantries are receiving a wider variety of foods that are relatively high in demand. For example, prior to trade mitigation, Food Bank for the Heartland, based in Omaha, Nebraska, was receiving between eight and 15 different products from USDA each month. Now, it gets between 20 and 25, including pulled pork, pork patties, pistachios and various nuts, said Brian Barks, president and CEO.

"We are grateful for the product we're receiving," Barks said. "It's good product and it comes with some associated cost, but quite frankly, we're in the business of helping people in need in Nebraska and western Iowa."

Among those extra costs for food banks are the logistical challenges of preserving perishable goods that China won't buy. For Food Bank for the Heartland and others, that's meant increasing freezer capacity and storage space. Holding on to perishable goods longer gives their resource-limited food pantry partners time to make space for the additional items.

Lafayette, Indiana's Food Finders Food Bank has saved on expenses like meat and produce, but it's also doubled its transportation costs to accommodate larger deliveries, said Jack Warner, director of operations.

"No matter where you save one place," Warner said, "it seems like something else picks up in cost."

People line up for breakfast at Shepherd's Table, a soup kitchen in Silver Spring, Maryland. Organizers say nonperishable goods received through a nutrition assistance program help to supplement the menu when food runs low.

Patrons line up outside a discreet entrance at Shepherd's Table, a soup kitchen here in Silver Spring, Maryland, before hourlong meal times. Organizers say nonperishable TEFAP items help to supplement the menu when goods run low.

A veteran with shoulder length gray hair who lives in subsidized housing above the kitchen said he thanked God for the hearty meals, which on a recent Monday morning included hard-boiled eggs, corn beef hash, leftover casserole, bagels, donuts, cream of wheat and apple crisp crumble. But there are certain foods you'll never get.

"You can't get steak and cheese here," said Alan, a chatty regular who declined to give his age.

Last fall, Food Finders received an unusually large delivery of shredded cheese, as in 30,000 pounds. Since then, its 33,000-square-foot warehouse—roughly three-quarters of an acre—is packed with oranges, apples and potatoes, sometimes stored anywhere organizers can find space for it.

"There are times when all my rack space is full in the cooler and all I have is space on the floor and even my floor space is full," Warner said. "I'd have to sometimes leave the potatoes out in the main area and turn my AC down to 65 degrees, so they don't spoil on me."

While it doesn't hurt to have more food in the food bank network, there already are proven programs in place, such as SNAP, or the Supplemental Nutrition Assistance Program, to address hunger in low-income populations. People often consider food banks as tools for preventing hunger, but it's also important to have a steady, well-functioning food and agricultural economy, said Wilde, the Tufts professor.

"If you wanted to remedy harm by helping low-income Americans, a strong safety net broadly would be my first recommendation, and good wage policies," Wilde said. "Additional commodities for food banks are nice, but they're fairly far down the list."

Print Citations

CMS: Simpson, April. "Food Banks Win in a Trump Trade War." In *The Reference Shelf: Food Insecurity & Hunger in the United States,* edited by Micah L. Issitt, 112-116. Amenia, NY: Grey House Publishing, 2021.

MLA: Simpson, April. "Food Banks Win in a Trump Trade War." *The Reference Shelf: Food Insecurity & Hunger in the United States,* edited by Micah L. Issitt, Grey House Publishing, 2021, pp. 112-116.

APA: Simpson, A. (2021). Food banks win in a Trump trade war. In Micah L. Issitt (Ed.), *The reference shelf: Food insecurity & hunger in the United States* (pp. 112-116). Amenia, NY: Grey House Publishing.

Tackling Hunger at Home and Abroad Because Our Food Policy Is Our Foreign Policy

By Dwight Evans
The Hill, December 4, 2017

For the first time in a decade, the number of hungry people on the planet is on the rise. The United Nations estimates the number of food-insecure people at 815 million in 2017—up from 777 million just two years ago.

At the same time, just 8 percent of people in low-income countries are covered by food-based safety net systems that could help the most vulnerable households keep food on the table when crisis strikes, according to a recent report by the World Bank.

There's a potentially timely solution to help address this critical gap in our hunger fighting toolkit: the 2018 Farm Bill reauthorization.

Every five years or so, lawmakers in our nation's Capital reauthorize a bill that combines support for American farmers with assistance for families struggling to access nutritious foods.

The Farm Bill is an important example of our country's deep reliance on one another, with neighborhoods nationwide coming together to ensure that no one—either at home and abroad—goes hungry, all while ensuring that agriculture producers have the tools needed to succeed.

One of the most well-known elements of the Farm Bill is the Supplemental Nutrition Assistance Program (SNAP), formerly known as food stamps. SNAP is among the most sophisticated social safety net programs in the world—and it works. In 2016 alone, the SNAP program pulled more than 3.6 million people out of poverty, many of them children. The program also has a genuine multiplier effect on the economy, which is why it played a central role in the 2009 stimulus efforts.

Some 71,182 households in the 2nd District of Pennsylvania became more food-secure in 2016 thanks to SNAP, according to the U.S. Department of Agriculture (USDA). Meanwhile, the number of Americans on SNAP is the lowest number in nearly six years, demonstrating the program's ability to graduate participants as our economy improves. Our country should be transferring these lessons learned at home to the growing number of fragile countries worldwide. We wouldn't go without a food-based safety net in this country; others shouldn't either.

Food policy is our foreign policy—and this year's Farm Bill cycle offers a unique opportunity to reinforce this idea. The next Farm Bill should expand the authority for the

The United Nations estimates the number of food-insecure people at 815 million in 2017—up from 777 million just two years ago.

USDA—particularly the Food and Nutrition Service—to provide technical assistance for the development of food-based social safety net systems in developing countries. In just one example, the Richard Russell National School Lunch Act is currently interpreted to limit the provision of USDA technical assistance to states and local schools. These authorities can be easily expanded—and now is the time to do so.

Ensuring global food security is an investment in our own national security. Almost 60 percent of the world's 815 million hungry people live in countries affected by man-made conflict. What is universally true about modern conflicts today is that they do not respect borders. What we saw in the aftermath of the 2007-2008 global food price spike is that countries with functioning safety net systems—equivalent to America's SNAP—were largely able to avoid the rioting and social unrest that occurred in countries without such social protection.

The 2016 Global Food Security Act emphasized the need to expand this form of support, but relative to other areas like access to markets and agricultural inputs— more traditional forms of food security assistance— this has yet to translate into significant gains abroad.

In many ways, functioning safety net systems are the long-term exit strategy for donor nations like the United States, protecting vulnerable people from shocks and ultimately contributing to the stability of our own nation. A loaf of bread to a hungry family might be one of the best tools in our toolbox to prevent the spread of terrorism.

The U.S. has a long bipartisan history of leading the global fight to end hunger— from the Marshall Plan in the aftermath of the Second World War to the Food for Peace food aid program that has reached over 3 billion people with lifesaving food grown by American farmers for over 70 years. This Farm Bill provides an opportunity to see that this legacy continues and that our successes at home are applied abroad in service to our future trading partners and allies. Food is the glue that keeps our neighborhoods united and strong both here at home and around our globe.

Print Citations

CMS: Evans, Dwight. "Tackling Hunger at Home and Abroad Because Our Food Policy Is Our Foreign Policy." In *The Reference Shelf: Food Insecurity & Hunger in the United States,* edited by Micah L. Issitt, 117-119. Amenia, NY: Grey House Publishing, 2021.

MLA: Evans, Dwight. "Tackling Hunger at Home and Abroad Because Our Food Policy Is Our Foreign Policy." *The Reference Shelf: Food Insecurity & Hunger in the United States,* edited by Micah L. Issitt, Grey House Publishing, 2021, pp. 117-119.

APA: Evans, D. (2021). Tackling hunger at home and abroad because our food policy is our foreign policy. In Micah L. Issitt (Ed.), *The reference shelf: Food insecurity & hunger in the United States* (pp. 117-119). Amenia, NY: Grey House Publishing.

5
Finding Solutions

By Linda, via Wikimedia.

Urban farms are one possible solution to food insecurity and lack of access to fresh produce. Above, an urban farm in Chicago.

Efforts to Combat Hunger and Food Insecurity in the United States

Food insecurity and hunger have been recognized as among the most significant problems in the United States for decades, and there have been many efforts to enact reforms. But most efforts fall short of the mark of eliminating hunger. To be clear, there is enough food to go around. A research report from the *Journal of Sustainable Agriculture* released in 2012 found that the world's farmers in that year produced enough food to feed 10 billion people, while the population of the world was around 7.5 billion.[1] The problem has never been that there isn't enough food, but rather that efforts to feed the hungry are complicated by the effort to profit from the production and distribution of food. For societies to end hunger, there needs to be a broad commitment to reduce food waste and to redistribute food to those in need. However, while large-scale efforts could, if handled correctly, have an important role to play, experts studying the issue have repeatedly noted that independent, local solutions are often more effective and produce additional beneficial impacts within communities.

Creating Food Oases and Meeting Community Needs

In the early days of American culture, independent churches and outreach organizations were most involved in combating hunger. The first "soup kitchens" and "homeless shelters" were organized by religious activists who saw, in their faith, a directive to help the less fortunate. This kind of organized social welfare has been at the core of America's efforts to combat problems, and local movements can be tailored to the specific needs or challenges faced by individuals in a specific community.

For many, the struggle to obtain adequate nutrition is more complicated than the process of finding adequate food. Affordable food outlets offer more affordable fare, but much of what the company produces is processed food, lacking in both freshness and nutrition. Though healthier options can be found in supermarket chains, such items come at a higher cost. Individuals operating on low-income budgets might therefore feel that they are unable to afford the healthier food options available. Further, many residents in low-income areas may lack the knowledge to make healthier choices and may lack the skills to prepare healthier and more nutritious meals. Years of reliance on processed, low-quality foods have created a schism in which access to and familiarity with healthier options has increasingly become a luxury lifestyle.

One of the proposed solutions for dealing with these issues is the establishment of neighborhood or community food co-ops. A co-op is business owned not by a corporation or group of investors but by members and employees. When making decisions about how the co-op will spend its resources or how the organization will function co-ops utilize a democratic model with members voting on various proposals. There are many types of co-ops, from industrial manufacturing to fishing, but the system is best known in the field of agriculture and, specifically, as a community-oriented substitute for the standard grocery store business model.[2]

In terms of combating hunger and food deserts, food co-ops have many advantages. Co-op's can, for instance, make purchasing decisions based on the desire to provide good quality food rather than through a cost-benefit analysis. Co-op members can also make decisions based on factors like sustainability or may shape their organization to focus on food produced locally, thereby utilizing the organization's resources to support other local businesses. These are decisions that large corporations typically do not make, because such decisions may limit profitability. Further, co-ops can and often do provide rudimentary nutritional guidance for customers, which can be accomplished by hiring employees who share a desire to promote better nutrition and well-being. In other cases, co-ops might offer other cooking classes or programs that teach consumers how to better utilize their food and avoid waste.

Co-ops are funded through the membership fees paid by members. If properly run, co-ops can keep costs low, but the cost of involvement is an impediment for some at the lower end of the income spectrum. One of the ways that states and the federal government can help to close this gap is through providing subsidies and other advantages to co-ops. Tax breaks and other subsidies can help co-ops to meet the mission of providing sustainable and nutritious food and can help to close the wealth gap in marginalized communities.

Food co-ops are just one of many ways in which local, community organizations and institutions can help with the hunger problem. Charitable organizations and groups that provide free meals or groceries for individuals or families in need fill an important niche in American society, helping to compensate for the nation's limited social welfare efforts at the federal and state level. Numerous studies have found that Americans donate more to charities than in most other nations, but this is largely because Americans are aware that the poor and destitute have no suitable options outside of charitable donations and service. In many nations in Europe, where social welfare systems are better developed and where rates of hunger and homelessness are lower overall, citizens feel less compelled to donate to charities directly because their tax revenues already support a number of state-run efforts to accomplish the same goals.[3]

Another local way to address hunger and food insecurity is by establishing local grocery stores. Unlike large retail chains, local stores can cater to an immediate community and can become part of that community, employing local individuals and drawing community members together. The high cost of food means that many smaller grocery store chains cannot compete with large-scale operations in terms of food costs, and this is one of the primary reasons that local grocery stores have been gradually disappearing from America's cities and towns. However, local grocery options can be restored and expanded through a combination of community investment and federal or state assistance. This is one of the arenas in which local and state policies can make a significant difference. States often provide subsidies to large grocery chains agreeing to establish outlets in low-income or underserved areas, but subsidies may be better directed toward independent stores. A 2019 bipartisan proposal in Kansas sought to provide subsidies to independent grocery stores operating in areas designated as "food deserts" around the country. Though the bill failed to pass through Congress in either 2019 or in 2020,[4] the idea of subsidizing independent grocery options has the support of a number of national hunger relief organizations and has managed to draw bi-partisan support in Congress. Such proposals could not only supplement food availability but also create opportunities for employment in vulnerable areas.

Addressing Larger Issues

While local solutions may be most effective in combating hunger locally, what can be done on the larger scale to address the underlying factors that contribute to food insecurity? One of the big ideas that has become popular in the 2010s and 2020s is the idea of reviving underutilized and "neglected" crops to fill empty niches in the food market.[5] For instance, in 2018 the BBC reported on a farmer in Malacca who was growing a berry called kedondong, a berry that was once used in Malaysian cuisine, as a preserved food or fresh, but that has been largely forgotten as produce markets shifted toward more familiar crops, most of which have a foreign origin. The global research enter in Malaysia known as the Crops for the Future (CFF) organization has embraced the mission of reviving forgotten crops to create more sustainable local agriculture and to provide work for a new host of farmers who can help bring these alternative crops to the market. One of the most important factors in this effort is that many of the crops grown at the CFF are local and thus agricultural programs based on those crops can be more sustainable.[6]

Evidence suggests that shifting to local crops can also benefit local plant and animal populations, which means that the cultivation of forgotten local produce and other food products can become an environmental boon, encouraging the preservation of ecosystems and animal populations to aid in the rapid production of these unusual food products. Even without the cultivation of forgotten crops, shifting from imported to local agriculture and food production can result in lowered costs for higher quality food and can reduce reliance on mass import and export systems that are unsustainable and ecologically destructive. Another flourishing area of research deals with how to use sustainable technology to manufacture food in vulnerable areas while simultaneously combating climate change. Combining efforts to fight climate change with efforts to expand sustainable food distribution is a noble goal that, if successful, would satisfy two important needs simultaneously. While this is a field that is just developing, it is likely that climate smart agriculture (CSA) might become a significant strategy of the future, especially as climate change devastates more of the world's agricultural communities while population growth intensifies the demand for food.[7]

There have been many other proposals for how global nutrition might be improved through innovative means. It has been suggested, for instance, that insects might be cultivated and used as a sustainable option for other proteins currently available on the food market. The cultivation of food insects would constitute, in many countries, a relatively new branch of agriculture, requiring far less space and resources to produce large quantities of nutritious foods as similar methods utilizing bird or mammal species. Likewise, a growing number of organizations have been promoting the expansion of farming into urban areas, utilizing empty lots, backyards, and even rooftop gardens to provide healthy food that can be used to supplement diets. The growth of urban agriculture over the past decade has been one of the most notable impacts of the "green cities" movement that has arisen because of public concern about climate change and unsustainable development. Urban farming initiatives can be combined with other efforts to improve sustainability through green architecture and sustainable urban development, but a robust urban farming culture also has the potential to make a dramatic difference to those facing hunger and searching for ways to afford more nutritious food options.

Hunger and food insecurity are complex issues, and there is no singular solution that can solve these broad problems. However, the infrastructure to produce enough food to feed the world's residents is already in place, meaning that it is possible to close the hunger gap and to provide food for Americans at every level. On the larger scale, making the American food industry more sustainable and shaping the evolution of the industry to favor public welfare over corporate profit is the ultimate goal for all those working to combat hunger and food insecurity. Close links between industrial lobbies and politics make this a difficult goal to achieve, and this is, in part, why local and community-oriented development efforts tend to be more effective. Though the world has long struggled to provide for those who fall into difficult circumstances, the wealth of innovation and ideas emerging from different countries around the world provides cause for optimism that this goal may someday be achieved.

Works Used

Baldermann, S., L. Blagojević, K. Frede, R. Klopsch, S. Neugart, and A. Neumann. "Are Neglected Plants the Food for the Future?" *Critical Reviews in Plant Sciences*, vol. 35, no. 2, 2016.

"Climate-Smart Agriculture." *World Bank*. World Bank Group. 2020. https://www.worldbank.org/en/topic/climate-smart-agriculture.

Holt-Giménez, Eric, Annie Shattuck, Miguel A. Altieri, and Hans Herren. "We Already Grow Enough Food for 10 Billion People…and Still Can't End Hunger." *Journal of Sustainable Agriculture*, vol. 36, no. 6, July 2012.

"H.R. 1717 (116th): Healthy Food Access for All Americans Act." *GovTrack*. 2020. https://www.govtrack.us/congress/bills/116/hr1717 .

Jha, Preeti. "Are Forgotten Crops the Future of Food?" *BBC Future*. Aug 21, 2018. https://www.bbc.com/future/article/20180821-are-forgotten-crops-the-future-of-food.

Paynter, Ben. "America Remains the Most Generous Place in the World—but

Barely." *Fast Company*. Oct 16, 2019. https://www.fastcompany.com/90417884/
america-remains-the-most-generous-place-in-the-world-but-barely.

"What Is a Co-op?" *NFCA*. Neighboring Food Coops Association. 2020. https://
nfca.coop/definition/.

Notes

1. Holt-Giménez, Shattuck, Altieri, and Herren, "We Already Grow Enough Food for 10 Billion People…and Still Can't End Hunger."
2. "What Is a Co-op?" *NFCA*.
3. Paynter, "America Remains the Most Generous Place in the World—but Barely."
4. "H.R. 1717 (116th): Healthy Food Access for All American Act," *GovTrack*.
5. Baldermann et al, "Are Neglected Plants the Food for the Future?"
6. Iha, "Are Forgotten Crops the Future of Food?"
7. "Climate-Smart Agriculture," *World Bank*.

Why Community-Owned Grocery Stores Like Co-Ops Are the Best Recipe for Revitalizing Food Deserts

By Catherine Brinkley
The Conversation, September 11, 2019

Tens of millions of Americans go to bed hungry at some point every year. While poverty is the primary culprit, some blame food insecurity on the lack of grocery stores in low-income neighborhoods.

That's why cities, states and national leaders including former first lady Michelle Obama made eliminating so-called "food deserts" a priority in recent years. This prompted some of the biggest U.S. retailers, such as Walmart, SuperValu and Walgreens, to promise to open or expand stores in underserved areas.

One problem is that many neighborhoods in inner cities fear gentrification, when big corporations swoop in with development plans. As a result, some new supermarkets never got past the planning stage or closed within a few months of opening because residents did not shop at the new store.

To find out why some succeeded while others failed, three colleagues and I performed an exhaustive search for every supermarket that had plans to open in a food desert since 2000 and what happened to each.

What's a Food Desert?

I'm actually rather skeptical that food deserts have a significant impact on whether Americans go hungry.

In previous research with urban planners Megan Horst and Subhashni Raj, we found that diet-related health more closely correlates with household income than with access to a supermarket. One can be poor, live near a grocery store and still be unable to afford a healthy diet.

Nonetheless, the lack of one, particularly in urban neighborhoods, is often a broader sign of disinvestment. In addition to selling food, supermarkets act as economic generators by providing local jobs and offering the convenience of neighborhood services, such as pharmacies and banks.

I believe every neighborhood should have these amenities. But how should we define them?

U.K.-based public health researchers Steven Cummins and Sally Macintyre coined the term in the 1990s and described food deserts as low-income communities whose residents didn't have the purchasing power to support supermarkets.

The U.S. Department of Agriculture began looking at these areas in 2008, when it officially defined food deserts as communities with either 500 residents or 33% of the population living more than a mile from a supermarket in urban areas. The distance jumps to 10 miles away in rural areas.

Although the agency has created three other ways to measure food deserts, we stuck with the original 2008 definition for our study. By that measure, about 38% of U.S. Census tracts were food deserts in 2015, the latest data available, slightly down from 39.4% in 2010.

That means about 19 million people, or 6.2% of the U.S. population, lived in a food desert in 2015.

Michelle Obama Makes It a Priority

The Food Trust was among the first to tackle the problem. In 2004, the Philadelphia-based nonprofit used US$30 million in state seed money to help finance 88 supermarket projects throughout Pennsylvania, which helped make healthy food available to about 400,000 underserved residents.

Our research followed the success as it drew attention nationally. Rahm Emanuel made eliminating food deserts in Chicago a top initiative when he became the city's mayor in 2011. And Michelle Obama helped launch the Healthy Food Financing Initiative in 2010 to encourage supermarkets to open in food deserts across the country. The following year major food retailers promised to open or expand 1,500 supermarket or convenience stores in and around food desert neighborhoods by 2016.

Despite receiving generous federal financial support, retailers managed to open or expand just 250 stores in food deserts during the period.

How to Grow in a Food Desert

We wanted to dig deeper and see just how many of the new stores were actually supermarkets and how they've fared.

I teamed up with Benjamin Chrisinger, Jose Flores and Charlotte Glennie and examined press releases, website listings and scholarly studies to assemble a database of supermarkets that had announced plans to open new locations in food deserts since 2000.

We were particularly interested in the driving forces behind each project.

We identified only 71 supermarket plans that met our criteria. Of those, 21 were driven by government, 18 by community leaders, 12 by nonprofits and eight by commercial interests. Another dozen were driven by a combination of government initiative with community involvement.

Then we looked at how many actually stuck around. We found that all 22 of the supermarkets opened by community or nonprofits are still open today. Two were canceled, while six are in progress.

In contrast, nearly half of the commercial stores and a third of the government developments have closed or didn't it make it past planning. Five of the

> **In addition to selling food, supermarkets act as economic generators by providing local jobs and offering the convenience of neighborhood services, such as pharmacies and banks.**

government/community projects also failed or were canceled.

A shuttered supermarket is more than just a business failure. It can perpetuate the food desert problem for years and prevent new stores from opening in the same location, worsening a neighborhood's blight.

Why Co-Ops Succeeded

So why did the community-driven supermarkets survive and thrive?

Importantly, 16 of the 18 community-driven cases were structured as cooperatives, which are rooted in their communities through customer ownership, democratic governance and shared social values.

Community engagement is vital to opening and sustaining a new store in neighborhoods where residents are understandably skeptical of outside developers and worry about gentrification and rising rents. Cooperatives often adopt local hiring practices, pay living wages and help residents counteract inequities in the food system. Their model, in which a third of the cost of opening typically comes from member loans, ensures communities are literally invested in their new stores and their use.

The Mandela Co-op, which opened in a West Oakland, California, food desert in 2009, is a great example of this. The worker-owned grocery store focuses on purchasing from farmers and food entrepreneurs of color. As a result of its success, the Mandela Co-op is expanding and supporting the local economy at the same time many commercial supermarkets are closing locations as the grocery industry consolidates.

Our study suggests policymakers and public health officials interested in improving wellness in food deserts should take community ownership and involvement into account.

The success of a supermarket intervention is predicated on use, which may not happen without community buy-in. Supporting cooperatives is one way to ensure that shoppers show up.

Print Citations

CMS: Brinkley, Catherine. "Why Community-Owned Grocery Stores Like Co-Ops Are the Best Recipe for Revitalizing Food Deserts." In *The Reference Shelf: Food Insecurity & Hunger in the United States,* edited by Micah L. Issitt, 129-132. Amenia, NY: Grey House Publishing, 2021.

MLA: Brinkley, Catherine. "Why Community-Owned Grocery Stores Like Co-Ops Are the Best Recipe for Revitalizing Food Deserts." *The Reference Shelf: Food Insecurity & Hunger in the United States,* edited by Micah L. Issitt, Grey House Publishing, 2021, pp. 129-132.

APA: Brinkley, C. (2021). Why community-owned grocery stores like co-ops are the best recipe for revitalizing food deserts. In Micah L. Issitt (Ed.), *The reference shelf: Food insecurity & hunger in the United States* (pp. 129-132). Amenia, NY: Grey House Publishing.

Neglected Crops Could Be Global Solution for Food Insecurity

By Daphne Ewing-Chow
Forbes, September 30, 2020

Globally, an over-reliance on a few staple crops, namely maize, wheat and rice, has resulted in limited dietary diversity—a leading cause of persistent malnutrition. These few foods represent more than half of the world's calorie intake and have typically played a central role in the fight against food security, but to no avail—hunger, inequality and non-communicable diseases continue to rise. Perhaps it is time to try something new.

Despite the fact that there are more than 30,000 identified edible plant species in existence, only 6,000 to 7,000 are used for food and only 170 are grown commercially, while approximately 30 species fulfil 95 per cent of the world's calorie requirements, as factory-style farming systems continue to contribute to the overwhelming degradation of the world's natural resources and contribute to 26 per cent of total global greenhouse gas emissions. (*Science*, 2018)[1]

What's wrong with this picture?

An over-reliance on a few genetically uniform, high yielding crops to meet global nutritional needs has hurt the environment, economies, communities and human health. Many neglected and orphaned crops are at a high risk of disappearing and 75 per cent of plant genetic diversity has been lost since the 1900's.

While conceptually we may recognise the need to consume crops that are climate adaptable, resilient and nutritious, we do not understand the urgency. The World Bank predicts there will be a rise of 70 to 100 million people who are living in extreme poverty this year, the World Health Organisation has just announced that there have been more than a million deaths from a pandemic that is killing the most vulnerable among us, and 132 million more people will go hungry than previously predicted—in 2020 more people will die from hunger than from COVID-19.

Do we have time to wait? Crop diversification holds the solution for each of these problems, and with thousands of largely untapped food species, the possibilities are vast.

Underutilized crops hold "underexploited potential for contributing to food security, nutrition, health, income generation and environmental services," (Echo Community) with untapped solutions for feeding the world in a nutritious, environmentally conscious and economically sustainable ways.

The Future Food-Tech Summit, held virtually in September, attracted delegates from the largest and most innovative food and beverage companies in the world. I had the honour of chairing a dynamic round table discussion on the subject of underutilized crops and how these can be introduced and commercialised within communities. Participants included C-suite executives, entrepreneurs, scientists and venture capitalists. A delegate from Kraft Heinz talked about how the food company is "rethinking" its ingredients and another from Ocean Spray OCESP +9.5% spoke about the agricultural cooperative's commitment to zero waste and using "all parts of the plant." There was a consensus that technology was key to revitalising underutilized crops.

> Underutilized and orphan crops are significant potential sources of food in the countries in which they are grown, providing income for the poor and nutrition in local diets.

But while the large-scale use of technology provides an excellent opportunity for large industrialised nations to create markets and economies of scale in food production, developing countries must use a grass roots approach to create cultural change and buy-in.

Peter Ivey, food security activist and Founder of hunger charity, Mission:FoodPossible (M:FP), believes that the solution to the world's food security crisis lies in something he calls MVPs or Most Valuable Produce. He says that there is a no one-size-fits-all approach to the food security crisis and that MVPs should be specific to communities, nations and regions "on the basis of geography, nutritional value, yield value, size of harvest, climate resilience, regenerative potential and socio-economic factors."

Ivey has a preference for orphan crops—sources of food that receive little commercial attention—such as yam, sweet potato, cassava and coconut in his native, Jamaica.

Orphan crops are often stigmatised as "poor man's food," particularly in post-colonial contexts, like the Caribbean. This perception is a major challenge from the perspective of commercial viability.

Mission:FoodPossible seeks to promote orphan crops or MVPs by teaching "food leaders" how they can make a variety of delicious, modern and waste free meals. Ivey, who is also a chef and food anthropologist, is currently working on a "zero-waste, regenerative, climate friendly, pro-food security" Caribbean cooking series which he hopes will play a role in achieving this objective.

In the Cayman Islands, Tillie's restaurant, located in the upscale Palm Heights hotel, has bestowed orphan crops with a chic and luxurious stature—just as nature intended. Inspired by local produce and farms of Grand Cayman, dishes such as sweet potato empanadas and local green plantain tostones with green mango sauce, combine world class dining with the warmth of home.

Underutilized and orphan crops are significant potential sources of food in the countries in which they are grown, providing income for the poor and nutrition in local diets, while being affordable and uniquely adapted to their indigenous environment. Policy-makers must recognise that an over-dependence on cash crops and mono-cropping have driven a food systems imbalance that has resulted in economic decline, environmental destruction and death.

We no longer have the luxury to keep doing "more of the same".

Print Citations

CMS: Ewing-Chow, Daphne. "Neglected Crops Could Be Global Solution for Food Insecurity." In *The Reference Shelf: Food Insecurity & Hunger in the United States,* edited by Micah L. Issitt, 133-135. Amenia, NY: Grey House Publishing, 2021.

MLA: Ewing-Chow, Daphne. "Neglected Crops Could Be Global Solution for Food Insecurity." *The Reference Shelf: Food Insecurity & Hunger in the United States,* edited by Micah L. Issitt, Grey House Publishing, 2021, pp. 133-135.

APA: Ewing-Chow, D. (2021). Neglected crops could be global solution for food insecurity. In Micah L. Issitt (Ed.), *The reference shelf: Food insecurity & hunger in the United States* (pp. 133-135). Amenia, NY: Grey House Publishing.

The Solution to Food Insecurity Is Food Sovereignty

By Jeongyeol Kim and Pramesh Pokharel
Al Jazeera, April 25, 2020

Human society faces a moment of reckoning. The coronavirus pandemic has brought humanity to its knees and bared its many faultlines. No country has been spared.

As scientists scramble to find a vaccine that could rein in the pandemic, many countries have imposed lockdowns requiring people to stay at home. But for many of the poor, this is a challenge.

Slum-dwellers, living in crammed shacks, cannot abide by social-distancing measures demanded by governments, nor can they follow strict hygiene, as access to running clean water is scarce. The lockdowns have deprived millions of daily wage workers in cities from their income, pushing many families to the verge of starvation.

People living in rural areas are also struggling. While many of us peasants continue to work our fields, we are finding it increasingly difficult to sell our produce. Governments have shut down local markets which has left many of our crops rotting in the fields.

Small-scale fisher-folk have also suffered. Even if they are able to get to their fishing grounds in the sea, lakes or rivers, they too are finding it difficult to distribute their fish. The same is true for pastoralists and family-owned dairy farms.

Small-scale livestock farmers and peasant families with domestic animals are also worried about finding enough feed for them.

While disruption of local small-scale food production has indeed been significant, the large-scale food industry which relies on international supply chains to function has been hit even harder because of travel bans affecting labour supply and international distribution.

Indeed, the pandemic has highlighted yet another ill of countries becoming too dependent on large international food industries. For decades, governments did little to protect small farms and food producers which were pushed out of business by these growing dysfunctional corporate giants.

They stood idle as their countries grew increasingly dependent on a few major suppliers of food who forced local producers to sell their produce at unfairly low prices so corporate executives can keep growing their profit margins. They remained silent as evidence piled up of large agribusiness contributing disproportionately more than traditional small-scale farming to greenhouse gas emissions and global warming.

Local peasant markets gave way to supermarkets, and big businesses and their commodity trading partners took control of the global food system, disregarding all principles of agroecology and food sovereignty.

The aggressive expansion of industrial food production has also increasingly put human health in harm's way. Apart from the overuse of chemicals and over-processing of foods, which makes them less nutritious and more harmful, it has also resulted in a major increase in zoonotic diseases–those caused by pathogens which jump from animals to humans (just like COVID-19).

Today, food security in countries around the world is increasingly tied to big industrial food production. Singapore, for

> **Countries like Nepal, Mali, Venezuela and several others have already recognised food sovereignty as a constitutional right of their people.**

example, imports some 90 percent of its food; Iraq, which used to be the breadbasket of the Middle East, also gets more than 80 percent of its food from abroad.

The dangers of this dependency on international food supply chains are now coming to the fore, as communities around the world are facing the prospect of hunger. The World Trade Organization (WTO) and the World Health Organization (WHO) have already warned of the risk of worldwide "food shortages".

The COVID-19 pandemic is pushing many to recognise the importance and urgency of food sovereignty–the right of people to determine their own food and agricultural systems and their right to produce and consume healthy and culturally appropriate food.

Countries like Nepal, Mali, Venezuela and several others have already recognised food sovereignty as a constitutional right of their people. Other states should follow suit. Food sovereignty of the people is the best defence against any economic shock.

It addresses the most urgent and pressing need of the people, which is to have healthy, nutritious and climatically appropriate food, grown in a locality or a neighbourhood, where they most likely know the people who produce it. Agroecological and localised peasant production of food respects and co-exists with our natural surroundings. It keeps away from harmful pesticides and chemical fertilisers.

The hard-wired competitive logic of a free market economy should stop defining international trade. Human principles of solidarity and camaraderie should determine global trade policies and networks. For countries where local production is impossible or gravely challenging due to climatic or other conditions, trade should rely on cooperation and not competition.

That is why, for years, peasant movements, such as La Via Campesina, around the world have campaigned and demanded to keep agriculture out of all free trade negotiations.

Any order that promotes life over profits must become the bedrock of human civilisation. We are not living in such a world now, but we surely can.

As the world reels under the fallout of a pandemic, now is the time to start building an equal, just and liberal society that embraces food sovereignty and solidarity.

Print Citations

CMS: Kim, Jeongyeol, and Pramesh Pokharel. "The Solution to Food Insecurity Is Food Sovereignty." In *The Reference Shelf: Food Insecurity & Hunger in the United States,* edited by Micah L. Issitt, 136-138. Amenia, NY: Grey House Publishing, 2021.

MLA: Kim, Jeongyeol, and Pramesh Pokharel. "The Solution to Food Insecurity Is Food Sovereignty." *The Reference Shelf: Food Insecurity & Hunger in the United States,* edited by Micah L. Issitt, Grey House Publishing, 2021, pp. 136-138.

APA: Kim, J., & Pokharel, P. (2021). The solution to food insecurity is food sovereignty. In Micah L. Issitt (Ed.), *The reference shelf: Food insecurity & hunger in the United States* (pp. 136-138). Amenia, NY: Grey House Publishing.

GMOs Are an Ally in a Changing Climate

By Emma Harris
Wired, April 1, 2020

Someone once told me you could survive on just peanut butter sandwiches and oranges. I have no idea if that's true, but the advice suggested a tasty lunch for a road trip. It was a freezing, foggy day last December, and I was preparing to drive from my home in Klamath Falls, Oregon, to California's Central Valley, the great agricultural heartland of a state that produces a third of the country's vegetables and two-thirds of its fruits and nuts. As I spread my peanut butter, I read the packages on my counter. My nine-grain bread promised, vaguely, that it was "made with natural ingredients." My oranges were "locally grown." My peanut butter jar assured me twice, once on each side, that the spread was "NON GMO." It was even "CERTIFIED NON GMO." The inspection must have been a rather cursory affair, given that there are no genetically modified peanuts on the market.

The grocery aisle is a testament to our attachment to "natural" as a signifier for all that is good. And as many consumers become increasingly concerned about global warming, there's a tendency to assume that these same labels also mean a product is good for the planet.

But unfortunately, the packages on my counter and elsewhere in my kitchen, like my fancy organic sauerkraut ("Our passion for healthy, natural living is reflected in all our products"), told me very little that was relevant to climate change. My bag of local (that is, California) oranges presumably required less fossil fuel to get to my store than if they'd been from Mexico or Spain. But beyond that, I knew nothing.

Some labels—like "natural"—don't mean *anything*. A USDA organic certification is meaningful: It says the food was grown without certain forbidden synthetic chemicals and wasn›t genetically modified. But the label in no way guarantees that the food was grown in a manner best for the climate. For one thing, many organic crops use more land than their conventional counterparts. When you clear land for crops, you often cut down forests—destroying a valuable carbon sink and turning it into a carbon leak. On the other hand, some conventional farming techniques use less land but rely on artificial fertilizer, which can make its way into the atmosphere as a potent greenhouse gas called nitrous oxide.

Which foods generate the fewest emissions? No federal certification will tell me that. And what's worse, even when consumers are presented with information relevant to climate change, they seem blind to it. One study suggested that, on average, "sustainability-conscious" American consumers will pay $1.16 more for a package of organic coffee, but they won't pay a premium for a less familiar "Carbon Footprint" label that quantifies the emissions associated with the product. This may simply reflect how 20 years of the organic label have conditioned public consciousness, but it also suggests something else: that our moral intuitions about food are out of whack with the demands of a crisis that is right on top of us.

This is a problem. Agriculture, including livestock and forestry, accounts for 24 percent of human-generated greenhouse gas emissions. We face a formidable challenge in the years ahead. We need to reduce those emissions and also sustain a growing population in a world of increasingly extreme conditions. And it would be nice if we could do it without expanding agriculture's footprint, so the rest of Earth's species can live here too.

To do so, we're going to need to abandon some of our attachment to what we perceive as natural, and not just at the supermarket. After all, we're not going to stop global warming merely by chasing after premium versions of food that only a few consumers can afford. We need to revise our thinking about food so that, as citizens, we can push for the regulatory policies that will meaningfully shift our entire food system's effect on the climate.

For my money, this system won't look like today's organic or today's conventional, but an evolving mix of both. As it happened, some important people—farmers and scientists—willing to cross these ideological lines lived not too far away. In looking around for people who are thinking deeply about climate change, I'd heard about Don Cameron, who farms a mere 7 hours and 45 minutes south of me. Hey, it's the West. That's practically a day trip.

Sandwiches packed, coffee thermos filled, I kissed my two children and husband goodbye and headed south on US Route 97, out of the high desert basin where I live. Many hours later, as I approached Fresno, the landscape had flattened and dried out considerably. I'd eaten three sandwiches, several oranges, and finished my coffee. Early the next morning, after a night in a hotel, I drove through the darkness to Terranova Ranch. This farm, where Cameron is the general manager, sprawls over 6,000 acres in the already hot and dry San Joaquin Valley, an expanse that is expected to become 4 to 6 degrees warmer by the end of the century.

At the appointed hour, I showed up at the farm shop, where workers were gathering for the day, snacking on fresh almonds and joking in Spanish. Cameron, silver-haired in cowboy boots and fleece vest, suggested a tour of his operation in his Range Rover Sport. Terranova grows about 20 different crops. You may have munched on its pistachios; its red jalapeño peppers end up as Huy Fong's Sriracha sauce. The farm grows most of its food conventionally, but 950 acres are organic.

Driving by the fields, I was struck by how blurry the lines were between Terranova's organic and conventional operations. Cameron grows certain crops organically in part because they pay better, but he has also incorporated some organic techniques into his conventional side because they work. Using chicken manure as fertilizer helped him add phosphate and potassium to his soil; owl boxes provide him with chemical-free gopher control.

Climate change is on Cameron's mind every day, he told me, because nearly every part of his operation is changing as a result. It was December, but splashes of red peppers missed by a recent harvest still lit up the fields. "We've been growing peppers late in the fall," he said. Ten years ago, they finished the harvest in September or October. "Falls are warm and springs are earlier."

Early hot days have begun to kill some of his tomatoes, and he's looking for new varieties that can take the heat. He worries about his pickers in midsummer. "We don't want them to get heat sick." One Fourth of July, Cameron picked peppers for a shift, taking over from an older woman who was feeling ill. "I picked for an hour; I thought I was going to die."

When I asked Cameron what new tools or technologies would help to cope with climate change, the very first thing he said was "drought resistance."

Worsening droughts are putting pressure on water in the valley. Groundwater levels are falling, and, to cope, Cameron has installed huge pumps, pipes, and channels to move water from the periodic floods on the Kings River onto his almond orchards and to recharge his aquifer. But what he really wants are crops that can thrive with less water, and he isn't too particular about whether they are bred the old-fashioned way or genetically modified.

In later winter many of the fields in the valley were expanses of bare, sandy earth; but along the edges were a few flourishing green shrubs, about knee-high. These were Russian thistles, better known as tumbleweeds. (Later, they will mature, detach, and roll away to disperse their seeds.) These plants, native to Eurasia, slipped into America with imported flax seed in 1873 and have thrived across the West. Cameron pointed to one of the bushes, emerald green without irrigation or tending. "That thing grows with no water," he said. "There's a gene out there that could really help us."

In other parts of the warming world, drought is the least of farmers' worries: They struggle with too much water, not too little. Rice—the staple of more than half of humanity—grows in water, but it's finicky. While rice roots are happy underwater, the plant's leaves can't tolerate it. (Seedlings need to be transplanted into flooded paddies at the right point in maturity.) A flood that covers the whole plant will kill it.

In Davis, California, 190 miles from Terranova, I met up with Pamela Ronald, a plant geneticist at UC Davis who has worked to solve this problem. Climate change is making floods worse in parts of South Asia, and in 2006, Ronald helped create a kind of rice that can survive submersion in water. By 2017, some 6 million farmers in Bangladesh, Nepal, and India were growing this rice. We talked in her cozy office, where a painting hangs on the wall of a man under a deluge of rain struggling to plow a field.

The history of agriculture is all about human intervention, taking plants and breeding them to produce a better yield or tastier fruit. Ronald sped up this process by using molecular tools to identify the genes that allowed a low-yield rice to withstand floods. Colleagues at the International Rice Research Institute in the Philippines then bred the submergence-tolerant variety with popular high-yielding varieties. They used genetic markers to screen the resulting offspring when they were seedlings, keeping only those with the right genes.

This creation, Sub1 rice, is not considered a GMO by many definitions, because no genes from other species were

> **There are 899 million acres of farmed land in the US. Farmers are a pragmatic bunch. If they are going to make changes, it has to pay.**

inserted into the plants. But Ronald encourages genetically engineering crops if it can do anything to mitigate climate change or help low-income farmers. "You want all the options on the table for climate," she says. She points to a transgenic form of eggplant that is also a hit in Bangladesh. It contains a gene from a bacteria that allows the plant to repel a particularly destructive moth larvae, which is thriving in a hotter world. Farmers who plant this GMO eggplant variety are able to cease sometimes daily applications of toxic and expensive pesticides.

Affluent, environmentally conscious shoppers often shun GMOs, as any stroll down a Whole Foods aisle will attest. Organizations of organic farmers have generally fought to prevent GMOs from getting an organic label, even for traits like drought tolerance. Critiques generally fall into three camps: the often high cost of engineered seeds, concerns about herbicides sprayed on herbicide-resistant GMOs, and vague worries about safety. As far as the first criticism goes, it is true that some GMOs require farmers to pay each year for expensive seeds, but that cost does not apply to crops developed by a nonprofit (as Sub1 rice was). The second applies only to the subset of GMOs that are engineered to tolerate glyphosate herbicide. (And to confuse things even more, some of the herbicides used before were arguably worse.) As far as safety goes, decades of scientific research has shown there's nothing especially different about genetically modified crops in terms of health or safety.

While most GMO crops are still either herbicide tolerant or pest resistant, more climate-change-ready traits are beginning to roll out. North American farmers are already planting corn engineered to be drought tolerant, though the seeds have mixed reviews. Genetically engineered drought-tolerant soybeans have been approved in the US, Brazil, Paraguay, and Argentina—where they are expected to be planted later this year. Corn engineered with drought tolerance and insect resistance for smallholder African farmers, funded by charitable entities, is aiming to be in farmers' hands by 2023.

With new, precise tools like Crispr gene editing, the potential is enormous. In addition to drought and heat tolerance, crops could be engineered to increase yields (and thus reduce agricultural footprints) and to be resistant to the pests and diseases that thrive in hotter climates.

The way Ronald sees it, we are in a crisis that demands every possible tool. Imagine that one of your loved ones had a virulent cancer, she says, and the most effective medicine was one that had been engineered in a lab. "You would never pull an option off the table because it was genetically engineered," she says. Why would we do so for our planet?

After a short walk through the UC Davis campus, I met up with Raoul

Adamchak—bearded, bespectacled, and clad in overalls and a wide-brimmed hat. Since 1996, Adamchak has overseen the Market Garden at UC Davis. He cares for seven picture-perfect organic acres with a rotating crew of undergrads. The core of organic farming, he says, it to nourish soil with composts and manures, cover crops, and creative crop rotations rather than unhealthy or environmentally damaging chemicals.

As students washed purple carrots and sorted ruby-red beets, I helped Adamchak harvest a few rows of gai lan, a slender vegetable with yellow blooms. Organic farmers and geneticists tend to live in different ideological universes, and there's little trust between them. But Adamchak thinks GMOs should not be banned from the organic label. If Adamchak has managed to be more open-minded, it may be because he spends a significant amount of time talking to one particular crop scientist: Pam Ronald, his wife, with whom he wrote *Tomorrow's Table*, a plea for a detente between the sides.

The combination of GMO crops and organic farming methods, he says, could be particularly powerful for farmers on small plots in low-income countries. If staples like corn could be engineered to fix their own nitrogen, resist pests, and survive heat, cash-strapped farmers wouldn't have to buy inorganic fertilizer or pesticides. And they wouldn't starve as the climate warms.

GMOs aren't the only solution, of course, especially for many parts of the world that would benefit more quickly from solar-powered irrigation or other low-tech improvements. And the fact that many GMO seeds must be purchased anew every year is another drawback. Partly this is because they are almost always hybrids. Hybrids are plants whose parents are different varieties of the same species. They are beloved by farmers because of what is known as hybrid vigor: the nearly magical ability for the plant to produce more edible food than either parent variety while also being harder to kill.

Unfortunately, the offspring of hybrids are duds, producing unpredictable crops. Scientists have been working on that too. Another UC Davis plant geneticist, Imtiyaz Khanday, stumbled on a way to tweak a single gene and make hybrids breed true. Khanday's hybrids create seeds that are clones of themselves—preserving all the benefits of hybrid vigor and whatever drought, flood, or pest tolerance the hybrids were engineered to express. He hasn't mastered the technique yet, but his breakthrough could theoretically work in all sorts of crops. Farmers could save seeds and replant. He hopes to see the first hybrid clones in farmers' fields in 10 years, but concedes, "I am being very optimistic about it."

On my drive back to Oregon from Davis, I started imagining what agriculture could look like if it were optimized for climate. What if, instead of focusing on inputs like chemicals or genetically modified seeds, we threw out the old rules and started looking at outputs—like greenhouse gas emissions, land and water footprint, pollution, worker and consumer health and safety? The result might look like a mashup of organic and conventional, depending on the context and the crop. High yield, low emissions. And it might borrow heavily from a style of farming that's become a bit of a buzzword recently: regenerative agriculture.

The core concern in regenerative farming is storing more carbon in the soil. This has a double benefit: Carbon dioxide is pulled out of the atmosphere, and the stored carbon helps nourish the soil. Practically, this means that farmers try to keep the soil covered and undisturbed as much as possible. They reduce or eliminate tillage—plowing, harrowing, or otherwise churning up the soil. They use crops like clover to keep the ground covered and add nutrients when the fields are fallow. They use composts and manures, plant perennial crops rather than annuals, and incorporate charred vegetation residue into the soil. All these practices can change the eco-system of the soil and its physical properties, making it better at holding moisture, nutrients, and carbon.

The number of acres in the US that are farmed without tilling increased from 96 million to 104 million between 2012 and 2017. During that same time, the amount of land planted with cover crops jumped from 10.2 million acres to 15.3 million acres. But consider this: There are 899 million acres of farmed land in the US. Farmers are a pragmatic bunch. If they are going to make changes, it has to pay. Back at home, I scheduled an interview with a startup called Indigo Ag, which has one nascent effort in that direction.

Based in Boston, with about $850 million in investment capital, Indigo pays farmers around $15 for every ton of carbon they add to their soil. Indigo claims that if every farmer boosted the proportion of their soil that is carbon to 3 percent (to-day's average is 1 percent), they could together draw down 1 trillion tons of $CO2$—"the amount of carbon dioxide that has accumulated in the atmosphere since the beginning of the industrial revolution"—a figure that some soil experts say might be a bit aspirational.

Indigo also tries to connect farmers with buyers who appreciate more environ-mentally friendly practices. Corn, soy, rice, and cotton are typically sold as com-modity crops at a standard price. Indigo Ag, however, runs a specialty marketplace where growers of crops who use sustainable practices—or grow grain to particular specifications—can sell their wares directly to food companies. "We think it is in-evitable that our food system shifts to being decommoditized so farmers get paid not based on inputs or principles"—as in today's organic farming—"but on com-mitments to nutritional quality and environmental protection," says Geoffrey von Maltzahn, Indigo Ag's chief innovation officer. Anheuser-Busch is buying 2.2 mil-lion bushels of rice through Indigo, specifying that the grain must be made with 10 percent less water, 10 percent less nitrogen, and produce 10 percent less emissions than generic commodity rice—producing a Bud you can presumably quaff with 10 percent less guilt.

Getting enough farmers to store carbon will require more than a few virtue-signaling companies to pay a premium for their crops. Bigger forces have to come to bear. Indigo hopes governments will eventually incentivize farmers to store car-bon—ideally setting a global price for every ton they are able to sock away, which von Maltzahn says would be "transformative to the economics of developing- and developed-world farmers."

Some policies already exist to encourage better agricultural practices. The US spends about $6 billion each year on programs that compensate farmers for environmental services like conserving topsoil or wildlife habitat. States run their own programs too. At Terranova, Don Cameron is tapping into one of these state programs to help pay for a 1.5-mile corridor of plants that support pollinators and insects that eat crop pests.

One can imagine a future where "farmers" spend just as much time and make as much money storing carbon and maintaining clean water and wildlife as they do selling soybeans and carrots. Farmers in such a system could become a real climate-mitigation force. Consumers would have a slew of new labels to choose from beyond organic: regenerative, carbon negative, wildlife friendly, and so on. In the best of all possible futures, one can imagine that these approaches become so mainstream that the labels simply disappear, because incentives and regulations ensure that all agriculture is producing safe, healthy food while simultaneously improving the environment.

In a system judged by outputs, not inputs, farmers could mix gene editing and automation with cover crops and compost and monarch butterflies and owls. They could create their own kind of hybrid vigor.

Planning the future of the food system made me hungry. When I got home, I chopped up some conventional orange carrots that Cameron had yanked out of the ground for me at Terranova and some of Adamchak's organic purple and white carrots and mixed them together. I drizzled them in olive oil from California groves, seasoned them with salt and pepper, and roasted them in the oven. My kids couldn't get enough.

Print Citations

CMS: Harris, Emma. "GMOs Are an Ally in a Changing Climate." In *The Reference Shelf: Food Insecurity & Hunger in the United States*, edited by Micah L. Issitt, 139-145. Amenia, NY: Grey House Publishing, 2021.

MLA: Harris, Emma. "GMOs Are an Ally in a Changing Climate." *The Reference Shelf: Food Insecurity & Hunger in the United States*, edited by Micah L. Issitt, Grey House Publishing, 2021, pp. 139-145.

APA: Harris, E. (2021). GMOs are an ally in a changing climate. In Micah L. Issitt (Ed.), *The reference shelf: Food insecurity & hunger in the United States* (pp. 139-145). Amenia, NY: Grey House Publishing.

Urban Farming Is the Future of Agriculture

By Patrick Caughill
Futurism, January 16, 2018

Surplus and Scarcity

The planet is growing more food than ever, and yet millions of people continue to starve worldwide. People are hungry everywhere—in the country, in the suburbs. But increasingly, one of the front lines in the war against hunger is in cities. As urban populations grow, more people find themselves in food deserts, areas with "[l]imited access to supermarkets, supercenters, grocery stores, or other sources of healthy and affordable food," according to a report by the U.S. Department of Agriculture.

New technologies are changing the equation, allowing people to grow food in places where it was previously difficult or impossible, and in quantities akin to traditional farms.

Farming at New Heights

Urban farms can be as simple as traditional small outdoor community gardens, or as complex as indoor vertical farms in which farmers think about growing space in three-dimensional terms. These complex, futuristic farms can be configured in a number of ways, but most of them contain rows of racks lined with plants rooted in soil, nutrient-enriched water, or simply air. Each tier is equipped with UV lighting to mimic the effects of the sun. Unlike the unpredictable weather of outdoor farming, growing indoors allows farmers to tailor conditions to maximize growth.

With the proper technology, farming can go anywhere. That's what the new trend of urban farming shows—these farms go beyond simple community vegetable gardens to provide food to consumers in surrounding areas. All vertical farmers need is some space and access to electricity, no special facilities required. Farmers can buy everything they need to start and maintain their farms online as easily as shopping on Amazon.

In fact, because it's so easy to access starting materials, officials don't really know how many urban farms are running in the United States. A 2013 survey by the National Center for Appropriate Technology (NCAT) received 315 responses from people operating facilities they describe as urban or suburban farms. However, federal grants for agriculture development show thousands of city-dwelling recipients, indicating that the number of urban farms is likely much higher.

"You have to look at these facilities in cubic feet as opposed to square feet. We can really put out a lot of produce from a facility like this," Dave Haider, the president of Urban Organics, a

> **Urban farms can be as simple as traditional small outdoor community gardens, or as complex as indoor vertical farms in which farmers think about growing space in three-dimensional terms.**

company that operates urban farms based in St. Paul, Minnesota, told *Futurism*. Technology allows vertical farmers to control the environment in their farms, enabling them grow a lot more in the same amount of space, according to a 2014 study in the *Journal of Agricultural Studies*.

Urban farms can grow more than just fruits and vegetables. Urban Organics grows three varieties of kale, two varieties of Swiss chard, Italian parsley, and cilantro, but uses the same water to raise Arctic char and Atlantic salmon—a closed-loop system often called aquaponics. Fish waste fertilizes the plants, which clean and filter the water before it goes back into the planters; excess drips into the fishtanks.

Urban Organics opened its first farm inside a former brewery complex in 2014. In the years since, it's brought food where it's needed most: to people in the food deserts of the Twin Cities. In 2014, *The Guardian* named the company one of the ten most innovative urban farming projects in the world.

"Trying to put a dent in the industry when it comes to food deserts is really one of the driving factors behind our first farm, which was actually located in a food desert," Haider said. Urban Organics sells its produce to local retailers and provides locally-sourced fish to nearby restaurants. "That was sort of a sort of our approach— let's try to grow produce and raise high-quality protein in an area that needs it most." As more people move to cities, problems like food scarcity might get even worse.

The vertical farm is also environmentally-friendly. Aquaponics systems result in very little waste. Vertical farming allows growers to use their finite area more efficiently, so we collectively can better utilize established space instead of creating more arable land, leaving more ecosystems intact. Placing the farms close to vendors and consumers means that fresher produce can reach tables with less reliance on trucks, which contribute to pollution and global warming.

What's the Harm in an Urban Farm?

As people all over the world move to cities, urban centers sprawl to accommodate them. Often, that means taking over former farmland to support more people. In New Jersey, cities like Camden and Trenton are becoming more populous as they convert into urban spaces.

Vertical farming can limit that sprawl. "Vertical farms can actually come into these areas to recolonize the city and to take spaces that have been removed from producing anything," Paul P.G. Gauthier, a vertical farming expert at the Princeton Environmental Institute, told *Futurism*.

But setting up an urban farm is often not an easy task. Finding enough space for an affordable price can present a significant obstacle for potential farmers. Vertical farmers also need to know how to operate more technology, including systems that control elements such as soil contaminants and water availability, that nature takes care of on a traditional farm.

Now, companies are popping up to help urban farmers get their facilities up and running. One Brooklyn-based company, Agritecture Consulting, helps people and organizations that want to start their own vertical farms to conduct market research and economic analyses, and to design and engineer the farm plans. The company has successfully completed more than a dozen projects to date, creating farms around the world, including some in the cramped confines of Manhattan and Brooklyn.

The benefits of urban farming practices extend beyond the tangible aspects of growing food in underserved areas—there's also a fortunate side effect of cultivating community. That's a big draw for organizations, including Urban Organics and Agritecture Consultants.

Growing Communities

Urban Organics opened a new facility this past summer. It's much larger than the organization's other locations, and could provide more than 124,700 kilograms (about 275,000 pounds) of fresh fish and nearly 215,500 kilograms (more than 475,000 pounds) of produce to the nearby area each year.

The former brewing complex in which the new farm is located is undergoing a revitalization, adding artists' condos and even a food hall, according to a press release emailed to *Futurism*. Haider is excited about the potential of the new facility and the impact it will have on the developing neighborhood. "Not only are we creating some good-paying, quality jobs with some medical benefits, but these are jobs that just didn't exist in the area prior to Urban Organics. And these are the things that excite us," he said.

This winning formula of bringing food and jobs to these areas can help build underserved communities. "Once that's done, we get to go out to identify the next markets and then do it all over again," Haider said.

Empowering individuals to get into urban farming can build community, too. Henry Gordon-Smith, the co-founder and managing director of Agritecture, has a side project called Plus.farm, a do-it-yourself resource website for individuals and small groups looking to start urban farms of their own. It's his passion project, his "labor of love," he told *Futurism*. "This is my way of not-so-subtly democratizing some of the best practices. It's a great way for people to create their own approaches, which is what I really want to see." The site allows farmers to come up with their own hacks—better lights, better sensors, better growing techniques—and share them on the site's forum. That's how an ancient practice like farming continues to improve with modern tools.

Farms of the Future

As people continue to study and tweak urban farming practices, we will continue to learn more about how they can benefit the areas surrounding them and the greater global community. Data on how urban farms directly affect their local communities may compel lawmakers to support and invest more in urban farms.

Gordon-Smith has planned another side project to this effect: an entire building or neighborhood to test urban farming technologies while gathering data. Though the location has not yet been decided, Gordon-Smith has already received a $2 million commitment from Brooklyn borough president Eric L. Adams; he has also taken his proposal to the New York City Council. The proposal is waiting for consideration from the Committee on Land Use, and there is no indication of when it will be decided.

Vertical farming, and urban agriculture in general, could be a significant boon for areas with the resources to invest, feeding residents and bolstering the local economy. Still, it's important to know that urban agriculture is not a singular solution to solve a massive problem like helping people access enough nutritious food. Gauthier, the Princeton urban farming expert, points out that there are a lot of important crops that simply cannot be grown indoors, at least not yet. "We'll probably never grow soybeans, wheat, or maize indoors," he said. "Vertical farming is not the solution for solving hunger across the world. It's not *the* solution, but it is certainly *part* of the solution."

Other efforts to combat world hunger grant people in poor nations more economic freedom by giving them lines of credit, or instituting basic income policies, like those being tested in Kenya. Education, social change, and female empowerment are all social initiatives that can help more people access the food they need to sustain themselves and their families.

Urban farms have the potential to change the world's agricultural landscape. Granted, we're probably not going to see a planet of supercities in which all farming is done in high-rise buildings. But urban farms can bring greater yields in smaller areas, increase access to healthy options in urban food deserts, and mitigate the environmental impact of feeding the world. That seems like enough of a reason to continue to develop and expand these transformative farming practices.

Print Citations

CMS: Caughill, Patrick. "Urban Farming Is the Future of Agriculture." In *The Reference Shelf: Food Insecurity & Hunger in the United States*, edited by Micah L. Issitt, 146-149. Amenia, NY: Grey House Publishing, 2021.

MLA: Caughill, Patrick. "Urban Farming Is the Future of Agriculture." *The Reference Shelf: Food Insecurity & Hunger in the United States*, edited by Micah L. Issitt, Grey House Publishing, 2021, pp. 146-149.

APA: Caughill, P. (2021). Urban farming is the future of agriculture. In Micah L. Issitt (Ed.), *The reference shelf: Food insecurity & hunger in the United States* (pp. 146-149). Amenia, NY: Grey House Publishing.

Bibliography

Avey, Tori. "The History of School Lunch." *PBS*. The History Kitchen. Sep 3, 2015. https://www.pbs.org/food/the-history-kitchen/history-school-lunch/.

Baldermann, S., L. Blagojević, K. Frede, R. Klopsch, S. Neugart, and A. Neumann. "Are Neglected Plants the Food for the Future?" *Critical Reviews in Plant Sciences*, vol. 35, no. 3, 2016.

Bartfeld, Judith, Craig Gundersen, Timothy Smeeding, and James P. Ziliak. *SNAP Matters: How Food Stamps Affect Health and Well-Being*. Stanford, CA: Stanford University Press, 2016.

Bordoff, Jason. "The Myth of U.S. Energy Independence Has Gone Up in Smoke." *FP*. Foreign Policy. Sep 18, 2019. https://foreignpolicy.com/2019/09/18/the-myth-of-u-s-energy-independence-has-gone-up-in-smoke/.

Brones, Anna. "Food Apartheid: The Root of the Problem with America's Groceries." *The Guardian*. May 15, 2018. https://www.theguardian.com/society/2018/may/15/food-apartheid-food-deserts-racism-inequality-america-karen-washington-interview.

Clapp, Jennifer. "World Hunger and the Global Economy: Strong Linkages, Weak Action." *Journal of International Affairs*, vol. 67, no. 2, 2014. https://core.ac.uk/download/pdf/144150286.pdf.

"Climate-Smart Agriculture." *World Bank*. World Bank Group. 2020. https://www.worldbank.org/en/topic/climate-smart-agriculture.

Coffman, Steve. *Words of the Founding Fathers: Selected Quotations of Franklin, Washington, Adams, Jefferson, Madison, and Hamilton, with Sources*. Jefferson, NC: McFarland & Company, Inc., 2012.

Costley, A. "Aging in a Food Desert: Differences in Food Access Among Older and Younger Adults." *Innovation in Aging*, vol. 2, no. 1, 2018.

Davis, Joshua C. *From Head Shops to Whole Foods: The Rise and Fall of Activist Entrepreneurs*. New York: Columbia University Press, 2017.

"Definitions of Food Security." *USDA*. Economic Research Service. 2020. https://www.ers.usda.gov/topics/food-nutrition-assistance/food-security-in-the-us/definitions-of-food-security.aspx.

Devitt, James. "What Really Happens When a Grocery Store Opens in a 'Food Desert'?" *NYU*. Dec 10, 2019. https://www.nyu.edu/about/news-publications/news/2019/december/what-really-happens-when-a-grocery-store-opens-in-a-food-desert.html.

Ewing, Jack. "United States Is the Richest Country in the World and It Has the Biggest Wealth Gap." *New York Times*. Sep 23, 2020. https://www.nytimes.com/2020/09/23/business/united-states-is-the-richest-country-in-the-world-and-it-has-the-biggest-wealth-gap.html.

Fadulu, Lola. "Trump Backs Off Tougher Food Stamp Work Rules for Now." *New York Times*. Apr 10, 2020. https://www.nytimes.com/2020/04/10/us/politics/trump-food-stamps-delay.html.

"Food Insecurity: A Public Health Issue." *Public Health Reports*, vol. 131, no. 5, Sept-Oct 2016.

Frndak, Seth E. "Food-Deserts and Their Relationship with Academic Achievement in School Children." *ProQuest Dissertations Publishing*. Buffalo: University of New York, 2014.

Gershon, Livia. "Where American Public Schools Came From." *Jstor Daily*. Sep 1, 2016. https://daily.jstor.org/where-american-public-schools-came-from/.

Green, Dymond. "Why Food Deserts Are Still a Problem in America." *CNBC*. Aug 20, 2020. https://www.cnbc.com/2020/08/20/trader-joes-kroger-walmart-super-valu-and-americas-food-deserts.html.

"Grocery Chains Leave Food Deserts Barren, AP Analysis Finds." *Chicago Tribune*. Dec 7, 2015. https://www.chicagotribune.com/business/ct-grocery-chains-ig-nore-food-deserts-20151207-story.html.

Holt-Giménez, Eric, Annie Shattuck, Miguel A. Altieri, and Hans Herren. "We Already Grow Enough Food for 10 Billion People…and Still Can't End Hunger." *Journal of Sustainable Agriculture*, vol. 36, no. 6, July 2012.

Horn, James. *1619: Jamestown and the Forging of American Democracy*. New York: Basic Books, 2018.

"H.R. 1717 (116th): Healthy Food Access for All Americans Act." *GovTrack*. 2020. https://www.govtrack.us/congress/bills/116/hr1717

"Inequality: A Persisting Challenge and Its Implications." *McKinsey & Company*. Jun 26, 2019. https://www.mckinsey.com/industries/public-and-social-sector/our-insights/inequality-a-persisting-challenge-and-its-implications#s_

Jha, Preeti. "Are Forgotten Crops the Future of Food?" *BBC Future*. Aug 21, 2018. https://www.bbc.com/future/article/20180821-are-forgotten-crops-the-future-of-food.

Karp, David. "Most of America's Fruit Is Now Imported: Is That a Bad Thing?" *New York Times*. Mar 13, 2018. https://www.nytimes.com/2018/03/13/dining/fruit-vegetables-imports.html.

Klein, Christopher. "How Did Food Stamps Begin?" *History*. Aug 27, 2019. https://www.history.com/news/food-stamps-great-depression.

Kretchmer, Harry. "Global Hunger Fell for Decades, but It's Rising Again." *We Forum*. Jul 23, 2020. https://www.weforum.org/agenda/2020/07/global-hunger-rising-food-agriculture-organization-report/.

Lowrey, Annie. "The Underemployment Crisis." *The Atlantic*. Aug 6, 2020. https://www.theatlantic.com/ideas/archive/2020/08/underemployment-crisis/614989/.

McMillan, Tracie. *The American Way of Eating: Undercover at Walmart, Applebee's, Farm Fields and the Dinner Table*. New York: Scribner, 2012.

McWilliams, James E. *A Revolution in Eating: How the Quest for Food Shaped America*. New York: Columbia University Press, 2005.

Milman, Oliver. "Earth Has Lost a Third of Arable Land in Past 40 Years,

Scientists Say." *The Guardian*. Dec 2, 2015. https://www.theguardian.com/environment/2015/dec/02/arable-land-soil-food-security-shortage.

Neumark, David, Junfu Zhang, and Stephen Ciccarella. "The Effects of Wal-Mart on Local Labor Markets." *Journal of Urban Economics*, Elsevier. 2008. http://www.economics.uci.edu/~dneumark/walmart.pdf.

"New Data Confirm Increased Frequency of Extreme Weather Events." *Science Daily*. Mar 21, 2018. https://www.sciencedaily.com/releases/2018/03/180321130859.htm.

"New Study: International Trade Supports Nearly 39 Million American Jobs." *Business Roundtable*. Mar 18, 2019. https://www.businessroundtable.org/new-study-international-trade-supports-nearly-39-million-american-jobs.

Nugent, Ciara. "The World Food Programme Won the 2020 Nobel Peace Prize: Here's How the Pandemic Has Made Its Work Even More Essential." *Time*. Oct 9, 2020. https://time.com/5898641/nobel-peace-prize-covid-19-hunger-crisis/.

Nunn, Nathan, and Nancy Qian. "The Columbian Exchange: A History of Disease, Food, and Ideas." *Journal of Economic Perspectives*, vol. 24, no. 2, 2010. https://scholar.harvard.edu/files/nunn/files/nunn_qian_jep_2010.pdf.

"PART 210—National School Lunch Program." *USDA*. Food and Nutrition Service. 2021. https://www.fns.usda.gov/part-210%E2%80%94national-school-lunch-program.

Paynter, Ben. "America Remains the Most Generous Place in the World—But Barely." *Fast Company*. Oct 16, 2019. https://www.fastcompany.com/90417884/america-remains-the-most-generous-place-in-the-world-but-barely.

Picchi, Aimee. "Trump Administration Still Wants to Cut Food Stamps." *CBS News*. May 15, 2020. https://www.cbsnews.com/news/food-stamps-record-trump-fights-usda/.

"The Population of Poverty USA." *Poverty USA*. 2020. https://www.povertyusa.org/facts.

The Public Health Effects of Food Deserts: Workshop Summary. National Research Council. Washington, DC: The National Academies Press, 2009.

Rude, Emelyn. "An Abbreviated History of School Lunch in America." *Time*. Sep 19, 2016. https://time.com/4496771/school-lunch-history/.

Schaeffer, Katherine. "6 Facts about Economic Inequality in the U.S." *Pew Research*. Feb 7, 2020. https://www.pewresearch.org/fact-tank/2020/02/07/6-facts-about-economic-inequality-in-the-u-s/.

Semega, Jessica, Melissa Kollar, Emily A. Shrider, and John Creamer. "Income and Poverty in the United States: 2019." *Census*. United States Census Bureau. Sep 15, 2020. https://www.census.gov/library/publications/2020/demo/p60-270.html#:~:text=The%20official%20poverty%20rate%20in,and%20Table%20B%2D5).

"A Short History of SNAP." *USDA*. U.S. Department of Agriculture. Food and Nutrition Service. 2021. https://www.fns.usda.gov/snap/short-history-snap#early%201980s.

Sweeney, Erica. "The Problem with School Lunch: How the Wealth Gap Is Shaming

Students." *Huffpost*. Aug 20, 2018. https://www.huffpost.com/entry/school-lunches-wealth-gap_n_5b72ee42e4b0bdd0620d0b43.

Temple, Nicola. *Best Before: The Evolution and Future of Processed Food*. New York: Bloomsbury Publishing, 2018.

Thompson, Derek. "Busting the Myth of 'Welfare Makes People Lazy.'" *The Atlantic*. Mar 8, 2018. https://www.theatlantic.com/business/archive/2018/03/welfare-childhood/555119/.

Tikkanen, Roosa, and Melinda K. Abrams. "U.S. Health Care from a Global Perspective, 2019: Higher Spending, Worse Outcomes?" *The Commonwealth Fund*. Jan 30, 2020. https://www.commonwealthfund.org/publications/issue-briefs/2020/jan/us-health-care-global-perspective-2019.

Tyack, David. *School: The Story of American Public Education*. Boston: Beacon Press, 2001.

"UN Warns Climate Change Is Driving Global Hunger," *UNFCCC*. Sep 12, 2018. https://unfccc.int/news/un-warns-climate-change-is-driving-global-hunger.

Varney, Vincent. "The Solution to Food Deserts Isn't More Supermarkets—It's Better Transport." *Here 360*. Sep 30, 2019. https://360.here.com/food-deserts.

Walsan, Ramya, Nagesh B. Pai, and Biju Rajan. "Food Deserts and Its Impact on Mental Health." *Indian Journal of Social Psychiatry*, 2016.

"What Is a Co-op?" *NFCA*. Neighboring Food Coops Association. 2020. https://nfca.coop/definition/.

"World Hunger Is Still Not Going Down After Three Years and Obesity Is Still Growing—UN Report." *WHO*. https://www.who.int/news/item/15-07-2019-world-hunger-is-still-not-going-down-after-three-years-and-obesity-is-still-growing-un-report#:~:text=More%20than%20820%20million%20people%20are%20hungry%20globally&text=An%20estimated%20820%20million%20people,of%20increase%20in%20a%20row.

Websites

Action Against Hunger

www.actionagainsthunger.org

Action Against Hunger is one of the world's largest and most important international nonprofit organizations in the fight to end world hunger and malnutrition. The organization began in France, but now has headquarters around the world, including in the United States. As of 2020, the organization is active in more than 50 countries and provides food aid for more than 13 million global citizens. Action Against Hunger also collects and publishes data to raise public awareness about hunger around the world and about the potential solutions that could be used to combat hunger.

Feeding America

www.feedingamerica.org

Feeding America is a domestic nonprofit organization, headquartered in Washington D.C., that operates food banks and other outreach organizations around the country. Feeding America was established in 1979, under the name Second Harvest, and has grown into the nation's leading food rights advocate organization. Many of the nation's private and community food outreach organizations receive funding and assistance through Feeding America and the organization lobbies at the state and federal level for legislation to protect children and families struggling with hunger.

The Food and Agricultural Organization of the United Nations

www.fao.org

The Food and Agriculture Organization of the United Nations is an international organization that promotes sustainable development and agriculture around the world. The organization also funds and supports efforts involving recycling, urban agriculture, and poverty reduction. FAO researchers produce a number of studies looking at different aspects of the international agriculture system and the organization distributes funding to private organizations working on programs designed to alleviate hunger and to promote nutrition in underserved communities.

Food Tank

www.foodtank.com

The Food Tank is an American nonprofit headquartered in New Orleans that organizes and manages annual "Food Tank Summits" in various states across the nation, each of which features a different theme related to the food industry or to challenges in addressing hunger and food insecurity. Food Tank conferences involve researchers, politicians, and activists from across the United States and the summits result in publications aimed at increasing awareness of issues involving hunger and food production. The Food Tank also supports research and publications involving issues such as urban development, sustainable and climate-smart agriculture, waste management, and public food policy.

National Cooperative Grocers Association
www.ncga.coop

The National Cooperative Grocers Association is a professional organization open to individuals involved in setting up or managing food cooperatives on a regional basis. The NCGA produces literature and data on food and farm co-ops and advocates for local cooperative grocery outlets and associations. According to the NCGA website, the organization represents 125 different co-op organizations in 35 states.

U.S. Agency for International Development (USAID)
www.usaid.org

The U.S. Agency for International Development (USAID) is an independent government agency created in 1961 that works on foreign development assistance programs. The USAID program has been enormously impactful in efforts to combat hunger nationwide as well as to organize sustainable development programs in various countries. The organization is heavily involved in funding development programs in Africa, Asia, and Latin America, and researchers funded by USAID also produce data on global hunger, development, agriculture, and infrastructure that can help guide U.S. policymakers working on agricultural projects.

U.S. Department of Agriculture (USDA)
www.usda.gov

The U.S. Department of Agriculture (USDA) is the branch of the federal government charged with developing and implementing all federal law related to food production, farming, and food industry infrastructure. The USDA supports a wide variety of research studies and programs designed to investigate different dimensions of the American agricultural system and offers free information from USDA studies through the department's official web page. The USDA also administers the Supplemental Nutrition Assistance Program (SNAP) that provides assistance for individuals and families facing hunger.

Index

type 2 diabetes, 39, 69, 79

U.S. Census Bureau, 6, 88-89, 130
U.S. Congress, 110
U.S. Department of Agriculture (USDA), 5, 59, 117
U.S. Environmental Protection Agency (EPA), 113
Udall, Tom, 54
UN Children's Fund (UNICEF), 21
undernourishment, 106
underutilized crops, 31, 133-134
unemployed, 4, 17, 19, 33, 35, 46, 89
unemployment, xi, 1, 4, 6, 10, 12, 14-20, 22, 31-32, 35, 89, 91-92, 100
unhealthy eating, 62, 79-80
unhealthy food, 78, 80
United Nations (UN), 11, 21-23, 106, 117, 118
United States Department of Agriculture (USDA), 5, 9-10, 13-14, 17, 19, 25, 33, 35-39, 43-44, 48-50, 53, 59-60, 65-66, 72, 78, 82-84, 89, 112-114, 117-118, 130-131, 146
urban agriculture, 126, 149
urban areas, 11, 59, 65-66, 126, 130
urban elitism, 80
urban farms, 75, 121, 146-149
urban food deserts, 79, 149
urban populations, 146

Vega, Yolanda, 18
vegetables, x-xi, 15, 18, 39-41, 62, 65, 67, 70, 72, 75, 78, 97, 112-114, 139, 147

Venezuela, 137
vertical farming, 147, 149
Vitale, Elyse Homel, 43
vitamins, x
Vollinger, Ellen, 35

wage stagnation, ix, xii, 4, 59
wages, xi, 6, 16, 18, 131
Wahlberg, Monica, 91
warming waters, 103-105
Warner, Jack, 115
water, xiii, 53, 73, 97, 99-100, 107, 136, 141, 143-148
weather, xiii, 99, 101, 103, 106-107, 146
welfare, x, 3, 5, 27, 29-31, 33-34, 59, 97, 100, 111, 123-124, 126
wheat, ix, 14, 115, 133, 149
Wilde, Parke, 112
wildlife habitat, 145
Wissmann, Mary, 74
Woodard, Stephanie, 52
World Bank, 117, 126-127, 133
World Food Programme (WFP), 21
World Health Organization (WHO), xiii, 21, 137
world hunger, xiv-xv, 21, 23, 101, 106-108, 149
World Trade Organization (WTO), 137
World War II, 29, 31, 114, 118

Younge, John Milton, 37

zoning rules, 66
zoonotic diseases, 137